Dry Aging
MEAT
at Home

Dry Aging
MEAT
at Home

Warren R. Anderson

Burford Books

Printed in the United States of America

10 9 8 7 6 5 4 3 2 1

Library of Congress Cataloging-in-Publication Data is on file at the Library of Congress

Contents

CHAPTER 1

An Introduction to Dry Aging

Ever since *Homo sapiens* began to kill animals and eat the flesh, meat has been aged unintentionally. The simple act of storing the flesh under certain conditions could cause aging similar to that which we do intentionally today. More often, however, the meat was stored under conditions that caused spoilage and putrefaction.

Certain kinds of meat—wild duck, for example—have been commonly aged in both Europe and the Americas for uncountable years. Usually, the ducks were neither drawn nor plucked, and this custom was usually called hanging rather than aging. The ducks were hung outside in a cool place until certain conditions were met: For example, they were left hanging until the feathers located just above the tail could be pulled out easily, or until the body of the duck that had been hung from the neck fell to the ground. Many waterfowl hunters still practice hanging.

The aging of other kinds of wild game has taken place in the past, and it is practiced in the present—the aging of various kinds of big game such as deer, elk, and moose, for example. But the aging has not been as well controlled nor as methodical as the process that has been developed in recent history.

The modern process for aging the meat of domesticated animals and domesticated waterfowl will be the main emphasis of this book, but the aging of wild game meat will be explored as well. However, to

1

the extent possible, the modern dry-aging process used for the meat of domesticated animals will be applied to the meat of wild animals. The reason for this is that the modern dry-aging process is much more likely to give consistent, satisfying, and very palatable results.

The basic result of dry aging the flesh of *any* creature remains the same—no matter if the creature is wild or domesticated and no matter whether the creature has hooves, wings, or paws. Dry aging, done properly, will normally result in flavor improvement, and this improvement could range between minor and fantastic. In the best cases, it is described as an appealing nutty, cheesy, and intensified meaty flavor and aroma. Additionally, dry aging can bring about increased juiciness and tenderness. The degree of the flavor improvement, increased juiciness, and increased tenderness will depend on conditions such as proper temperature control, humidity control, and the appropriateness of the dry-aging time for the variety of meat being processed.

Because modern dry-aging techniques will be used, this book *will not suggest*, for example, that an un-eviscerated duck be hung by the neck in a cool place until decomposition causes the body to fall to the ground. Instead, there will be instructions on how to dry age a plucked wild duck (or plucked wild duck breasts) in a sanitary refrigerator whose internal chamber temperature and humidity are both monitored and controlled. The goal will be to dry age wholesome and wonderfully delicious wild duck successfully every time, and the process used to dry age a wild duck will be the same modern process that we will use for a domesticated duck. In short, in this book the modern dry-aging process will be used for the meats of all animals and birds whether they are domesticated or wild.

The practice of methodically and intentionally dry aging beef has existed for quite some time. (The meat purveyors DeBragga & Spitler of Manhattan claim to have been dry aging beef commercially for over 90 years.) Surprisingly, however, it was not until the 1950s that the popularity of dry-aged beef increased rapidly. This practice spread rapidly because the meat and restaurant industry realized that the beef would become *dependably* more tender and flavorful if it were hung in a clean environment that had a controlled temperature, suitable humidity range, and steady airflow. Of course, this increased the cost of the beef, but the improvement in quality made the higher cost acceptable in the 1950s. A relatively short time later, in the early 1960s, the meat industry developed the practice of vacuum packing the freshly slaughtered beef (and some other meats) in strong plastic bags and then "aging" that meat in those airtight bags while it was under refrigeration. This practice was called *wet aging* and the previous aging came to be called *dry aging*. *Wet aging, therefore*, is nothing more than letting the refrigerated meat mature in airtight vacuum bags and natural juices for at least a few days. This wet aging does make the meat more tender, but the change in flavor is nonexistent compared with that produced by dry aging.

Because the wet-aging process required less labor, less time, less space, and no airflow control, and it did not result in the 15 to 25 percent weight loss caused by dry aging, it soon almost completely replaced the dry aging of beef. In the early 1960s, the higher profit margin and the lower price per pound were deemed more important than tenderness and taste.

In the 1980s, there was a resurgence in the dry aging of beef on the commercial level, and the number of white-tablecloth restaurants and high-end grocers selling dry-aged beefsteaks increased substantially. This development was probably influenced by an improving economic environment; there were enough deep-pocket patrons available to make dry-aged steak restaurants a lucrative business despite the increased meat-processing cost. Nevertheless, the wet-aged beef continued to be popular in restaurants and grocery stores because there were also numerous "shallow-pocket" customers.

Several factors contribute to the high cost of dry-aged beef. Drying and shrinkage result in a volume reduction and a weight loss, resulting in less consumable meat. In addition, dry aging produces a hard, dry, crust-like rind on the surface of the meat, which must be trimmed and discarded. A larger storage room is required, and air circulation, temperature, and humidity control must be managed. All of this, taken together, increases the overall cost to bring the meat to market. Obviously, dry-aged beef will rarely be on the shopping list of bargain-hunting grocery shoppers.

The cost to produce dry-aged meat commercially will always put this retail product beyond the reach of most people. Nevertheless, most people who want dry-aged meat can produce it themselves at home at a price they can afford.

Even though dry aging at home will take place in a refrigerator rather than a huge, professional aging chamber, the professional dry-aging environment can be duplicated rather well in the refrigerator. And if all of the basic conditions and features of the commercial dry-aging environment are duplicated, it is reasonable to believe that the quality of the dry aging will also be duplicated. The purpose of this book is to show how to do this.

ABOUT THIS BOOK

A few years ago, I decided to learn how to dry age meat at home. I have had considerable experience as a meat- and food-processing hobbyist and have had two books published on meat processing: *Mastering the Craft of Smoking Food* and *Mastering the Craft of Making Sausage*.

From the beginning of the time when my interest in dry aging was first sparked, I wanted to learn how to dry age the meat of various domesticated critters besides beef cattle: lamb, goat, duck, and goose, for example. Beef, of course, is the most commonly dry-aged meat, and I wanted to learn how to produce the popular dry-aged beef-steaks and beef roasts. However, instead of always using the expensive *prime grade* beef (first grade) that is served in the fancy steakhouses, I wanted to learn how to make delicious and tender dry-aged beef with the more affordable *choice grade* beef (second grade) or *select grade* beef (third grade). (Choice grade beef is the grade most commonly offered in American grocery stores.) I also wanted to make dry-aged beef with even *more economical cuts* of beef—top sirloin instead of sirloin, for example.

After mastering the dry aging of meat from domesticated animals, I intended to apply the same techniques to the dry aging of various kinds of wild game.

When I started to do the research necessary to learn the subject, the first problem I encountered was that I could not find even one book that explained how to dry age meat at home. I could not even find evidence of such a book having ever been published.

What I did find was snippets of information (and misinformation) about these subjects on the Internet. Some of the Internet postings were written by professionals who seemed more intent on advertising their dry-aging businesses than on describing how a person could accomplish dry aging at home. Other people who gave information were well intentioned and were sincerely trying to be helpful, but their lack of experience, and lack of knowledge of the scientific principles, meant that not all of the instructions produced the intended results.

Despite this lack of good information on how to proceed, I forged ahead. Initially, the results were a hodgepodge of discoveries and failures. The causes for the failures had to be investigated so that preventive steps could be taken. The reasons for successes had to be understood so that those procedures and techniques could be perpetuated.

Gradually, I did accomplish what I set out to do: I gained the experience and acquired the technical knowledge that enabled me to dry age the above-mentioned products consistently and dependably. After reaching this goal, I decided to share this experience and knowledge; I felt that a manual-like book might be welcomed by other people who wanted to improve the taste and tenderness of meat by learning *Dry Aging Meat at Home.*

CHAPTER 2

Equipment

Good-quality equipment, used properly, will produce good dry-aging results—and considering the price of meat these days, good results are important. Although good equipment is critical, good equipment for dry aging need not be expensive. I bought a sec-ondhand refrigerator and all of the refrigerator-related equipment indicated below for about $100; these are the most important dry-aging equipment items.

DEDICATED REFRIGERATOR

The refrigerator is, certainly, the most important equipment item. It provides the required clean environment, a narrow cold-temperature range, and an acceptable relative humidity range. Dry aging at home is, essentially, nothing more than storing a big hunk of meat (*sub-primal* or *primal cut*) in such a controlled environment for a period of a few days to a few weeks—or even longer than two months.

A *primal cut* of meat is a basic and initial division of an animal carcass. If a primal cut is further divided according to the traditional butchering practices, the resulting parts are usually designated as *sub-primal cuts*. The size of the animal and the local butchering practices will determine the size of primal and subprimal cuts, but these words are never used for a cut considered an individual serving.

For the following reasons, *it is important that the refrigerator be used only for dry aging; it should be a dedicated refrigerator.*

- If the refrigerator is used for common daily living purposes, it will likely be opened very frequently, and this will interfere with temperature control and the stability of the relative humidity. It will also provide increased opportunity for the entry of harmful bacteria and mold spores.
- If other food items (onions, for example) are stored with the dry-aging meat, the meat will likely absorb those odors. The fact that dry-aging meat is normally uncovered makes the meat even more susceptible to tainting by foul odors. Consequently, if the refrigerator is used only for dry aging, it is much less likely that the meat will become malodorous.
- Conversely, some food items (butter and cheese, for example) are notorious for *absorbing* refrigerator odors. These food items, if stored with the aging meat, will absorb its odors. The smell of dry-aging meat is not necessarily bad, but it does not complement the taste of items such as butter and cheese.
- The importance of good air circulation around all surfaces of the dry-aging meat is explained in numerous places in this book. Obviously, if the refrigerator is used for storage of extraneous foodstuffs, those items will interfere with free circulation of the air.
- A refrigerator used for dry aging must be clean, and it should be as free as possible from bacteria and mold spores. If the inside of the refrigerator is not clean, the aging meat (which remains uncovered in the refrigerator for many days or several weeks) may become contaminated. For this reason, the inside of the refrigerator should be cleaned and sterilized before *each* dry-aging session. Also, because food items other than the aging meat *can introduce* microorganisms, they should not be stored with the meat.

DESIRABLE REFRIGERATOR FEATURES

This book was written for those who want to dry age meat at home. Consequently, the refrigerator described here is suitable for the average person to dry age meat in an average residential setting. If the refrigerator described below does not meet your requirements in terms of size or some other consideration, select one that does. As long as the refrigerator maintains the acceptable temperature range and has the desirable features mentioned below, it should be acceptable.

Refrigerators come in many sizes and shapes, and there is a wide price range. A used refrigerator in good condition, as described here, can be bought on Craigslist, for example, for about $50 or $60.

Most homes can accommodate a mini refrigerator (also called a *dorm refrigerator*) in one of their rooms. If the capacity of this small refrigerator is 4 to 5 cubic feet (0.113–0.141 cubic meter), the two available open shelves will provide enough room for two large cuts of meat, and most people find this to be adequate. These mini refrigerators are normally about 16 inches (40.6 cm) wide from the left to the right inside walls. This means that each cut of meat can be about 14 inches (35.5 cm) long; this will allow 1 inch (2.5 cm) of open space on each end of the meat for the unrestricted airflow required for drying the meat surface. If the available shelf space inside a mini fridge is not adequate, buy a larger model that meets the overall requirements.

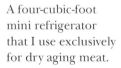

A four-cubic-foot mini refrigerator that I use exclusively for dry aging meat.

The temperature dial is visible near the upper left corner of the photo. The frost on the freezer compartment represents an accumulation from a 60-day dry aging session. The white, slotted tray is the drip tray.

The original refrigerator racks were glass. They were immediately replaced with wire racks from another used refrigerator. (Glass racks are unsuitable because they hinder air circulation.) Two wooden supports were required to make them usable.

Below is a list of desirable refrigerator features. These items are not necessarily listed in order of importance.

- Single-door construction is best. A separate freezing compartment is not required for dry aging, so a dedicated freezing compartment with a separate door is a waste of space.
- An inbuilt, adjustable, analog or digital temperature control is required. The refrigerator must be adjusted to maintain a range of about 34 to 38°F (1–3°C). (*Note:* It is helpful to keep in mind that the temperature-control device in a refrigerator is purposefully designed to maintain an *approximate temperature range, not a certain temperature point.* The control device is engineered in this way to prevent the refrigerator from undesirably cycling on and off too frequently, causing unnecessary wear and tear and a shorter life span.)
- Wire racks (shelves), or equivalent shelves that permit *unimpeded* airflow are required because all surfaces of the meat should dry uniformly. Glass shelves obstruct the flow of air and they should never be used; they prevent uniform drying of the meat and cause temperature variation inside the refrigerator. Any kind of shelves that impede the airflow more than wire shelves are not acceptable. The meat must set *directly* on the wire racks so that the airflow to all surfaces of the meat is *unimpeded.* If the meat is setting on a plate, a dish, or even waxed paper, the part that contacts the surface of such an item will remain damp and begin to rot: Impeded airflow can cause you to throw away a large and very expensive hunk of meat.
- Automatic defrost is undesirable because the defrost system usually turns on daily and causes an undesirable temperature rise above 38°F (3°C). For automatic defrost refrigerators, this daily temperature rise is required to accomplish defrosting of the evaporator coils. (Mini refrigerators with *manual* defrost are common and easy to find. This type of refrigerator can be defrosted manually between dry-aging sessions.)

REFRIGERATOR-RELATED EQUIPMENT

The internal temperature of a refrigerator used for dry aging is *very* important because the proper temperature range retards spoilage while the dry aging is progressing. A properly designed thermometer is required to monitor temperature changes and indicate when occasional adjustment is required. A temperature adjustment dial will likely be located in the upper part of the refrigeration compartment. This compartment should be maintained within a range of about 34 to 38°F (1–3°C). (When the temperature dial is used to change the average temperature in the refrigerator, allow about one day for the new temperature to stabilize.)

Any of several types of thermometers can be used for refrigeration-compartment monitoring. However, each type provides advantages and disadvantages, so you may be more comfortable with a specific type, or you may be most comfortable using two types at the same time. The various types of thermometers that can be employed, together with an explanation of their merits and drawbacks, are explored below.

When considering the merits of using one of the various thermometers in the refrigerator, it is important to understand that the *average* temperature should be kept in the 34 to 38°F range (1–3°C). If the temperature goes a little under 34° (1°C) or a little over 38° (3°C) for a short time, that is quite acceptable.

Analog Refrigerator Thermometer

The easiest and most economical way to measure refrigerator-compartment temperature is to use an inexpensive analog refrigerator thermometer. They can be purchased for $3 to $7. Because these thermometers take an hour or so to stabilize, they should be left in the refrigerator permanently so the temperature can be monitored at will.

The analog refrigerator thermometer pictured here, or the equivalent, will do the job: This is the *Taylor 5924 Analog Refrigerator/Freezer Dial Thermometer.*

An analog refrigerator thermometer is specially designed so that the reading will not change the moment the door is opened and air (of a different temperature) enters. It will take 15 seconds or so before the thermometer begins to register a change. (The temperature-sensing device is buried in material that absorbs and releases heat

An analog refrigerator thermometer. The diameter is about three inches (about eight cm). The temperature reading changes very slowly when the refrigerator door is opened.

slowly; the temperature changes are thus buffered.) During that time, the thermometer will show the temperature of the chamber *before* the door was opened. Any hardware or culinary store will stock them, or they can be ordered on the Internet.

The good points about this kind of thermometer are that it is inexpensive, and that its reading will remain the same for 15 seconds or so after the door is opened. The two bad points are that the door must be opened to check the temperature, and that the thermometer does not indicate an *average* temperature. (In addition to causing fluctuations of the refrigerator temperature, opening the door frequently can introduce mold spores and bacteria. It can also change the relative humidity.)

Analog Stem Thermometers

Analog stem thermometers are available with a dial diameter of less than 1 inch (2.5 cm), or slightly greater than 2 inches (5.1 cm). The stem is about 6 inches (15 cm) long. The smaller type is available for less than $6. They function in essentially the same way as the analog refrigerator thermometer except for the fact that any difference in the ambient temperature is registered rapidly because there is no built-in buffer. This is unacceptable because opening the door of the

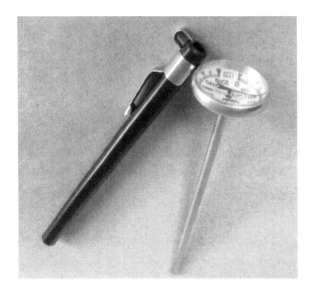

An analog mini-dial stem thermometer. The diameter is about one inch (about 2.5 cm) and the length is five inches (about 12.5 cm).

refrigerator is likely to cause a sudden change in the dial reading, thus making it impossible to know the internal temperature of the refrigerator with the door closed.

However, if the stem of the thermometer is inserted in a glass of water, this jury-rigged setup functions better than the previously described analog refrigerator thermometer. This is because the temperature of the water in the glass is better at indicating the recent average temperature of the refrigerator. (The water in the glass absorbs and releases heat slowly, and this provides an excellent averaging effect for the temperature changes.) The more water in the glass, the greater the averaging effect.

The bad points are similar to those of the analog refrigerator thermometer: The door must be opened to check the temperature, and opening the door not only causes a change in the chamber temperature but can also introduce mold spores and bacteria. It can change the relative humidity as well.

Wireless, Digital Electronic Thermo-Hygrometer

I feel that a *wireless, digital electronic thermo-hygrometer* is the best instrument for monitoring both the internal temperature *and* the internal relative humidity of the dry-aging refrigerator. You can purchase the following two-piece kit for around $30: *Meade Wireless*

The two-piece thermo-hygrometer set. The white device on the right is the transponder. It is placed in the refrigerator. The second part, the digital monitor, may be placed up to 100 feet away.

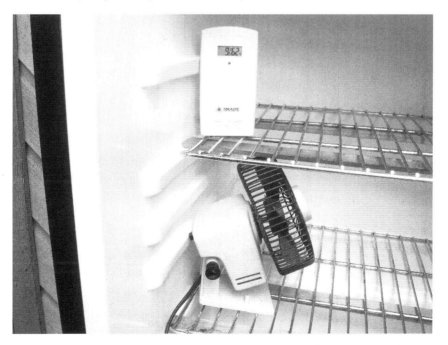

The transponder is placed on one of the refrigerator racks, and one of the air circulation fans is placed on another.

Indoor/Outdoor Thermo-Hygrometer and Transponder TM005X-M. (*Meade* is the brand name.)

This kit consists of two parts. The first part is the electronic sensor and signal transmitter (also known as a *transponder*). The transponder is housed in a white plastic case and is placed in the refrigerator. The second part, the digital monitor, can be placed and used at a distance within about 100 feet (about 30 meters). Obviously, this ability to monitor both the internal temperature *and* relative humidity leisurely, and at a considerable distance from the refrigerator, is a great convenience. For example, the monitor can be placed in the living room, and the refrigerator can be placed several rooms away at any distance within about 100 feet (about 30 meters). (Be sure that the digital monitor is not placed in front of a TV remote control device: Signals emanating from a TV remote control will interfere with reception of the signals from the transponder in the refrigerator. The Meade owner's manual explains this in detail.)

The main disadvantage is that there is no way to buffer the changes in the temperature that occur when the refrigerator compressor cycles on and off in order to maintain the selected temperature range. Consequently, the monitor will always show the current temperature reading. This presents no problem as long as the *average* temperature is kept in the 34 to 38°F (1–3°C) range.

Furthermore, it should be kept in mind that occasional readings on the digital monitor of 40°F (4.4°C) or 33°F (0.6°C) (for example) need not cause consternation. This might happen even if the refrigerator doors have not been opened for a long time. These small aberrations are caused by the intentional design of the compressor-cycling-control device (thermostat) built into the refrigerator to prevent excessively frequent cycling and will not cause a problem. The extent of the aberrations will likely vary among different refrigerator models.

Also, keep in mind that the substantial thermal retention properties of the large mass of meat will likely result in an unmeasurable change in the temperature of the meat despite the temperature fluctuations inside of the refrigerator. The temperature of the meat is, after all, of primary consideration, and if the temperature of the meat remains within the 34 to 38°F (1–3°C) range, there is no need to be concerned about temporary temperature aberrations in the refrigerator. (It is unnecessary, but if you wish, the thermal retention properties of the meat can be observed from the outside of the refrigerator by inserting the cable probe of a digital thermometer in the meat and making observations on the monitor setting on top of the fridge. The digital thermometer with cable probe is described in the next section.)

Monitoring with this *Meade* brand instrument helps to make sure that the proper ranges of temperature and humidity are maintained, and this monitoring can be accomplished while watching television, reading a book, playing cards, or making plans for the next dry-aging session. One helpful suggestion about using the monitor is to pay attention to the number used to indicate changes in the temperature. If the value of the *decimal* part of this number is *increasing*, this means, obviously, that the temperature is rising. Conversely, a *decrease* in that *decimal digit* means that the temperature is falling. This, of course, is common sense, but you will find that it is *very important and useful* to know if the temperature is rising or falling. For example, if the temperature is a bit too high, but it's falling, you need not be overly concerned. On the other hand, if the temperature is a bit too high and also rising, you need to monitor the situation and try to isolate the cause. Also, please keep in mind that humidity will always rise when temperature falls, and vice versa. (When temperature falls, the air volume is reduced, and when the air volume is reduced, the moisture in that air becomes more concentrated.)

Again, it must be stressed that the *average* temperature and humidity is important: Temporary and minor variations from the desired ranges should not be cause for concern.

Digital Thermometers with Cable Probes

Digital cooking thermometers with a cable and a probe are most commonly used to monitor the internal temperature of meat and other foods while they are cooking. However, these cooking thermometers are also very useful for monitoring the temperature inside the refrigerator. They eliminate the need to open the refrigerator to check the temperature. Next to the *wireless, digital electronic thermohygrometer* described above, *digital cooking thermometers with a cable and a probe* may be the best instruments for monitoring the refrigerator temperature. They can be found wherever kitchen equipment is sold. Simply put the probe in a glass of water in the same way as

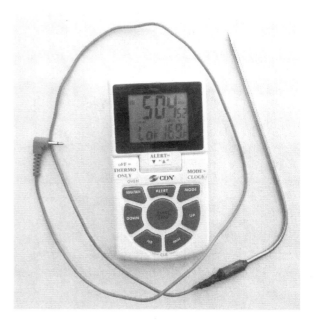

Digital thermometer
with cable probe.
Any brand will do.
This brand is a CDN,
Model DTTC-W
(*CDN* means *Compo-
nent Design Northwest.*
W means *white.*)

indicated in the section *Analog Stem Thermometers* (above), and then feed the probe cord out of the refrigerator door and set the monitor on top of the refrigerator. The probe cable is thin, so the rubber gasket on the refrigerator door will fit snugly over it as it exits from the refrigerator chamber.

The internal temperature of the refrigerator can be checked at glance by looking at the digital thermometer monitor on the top of (or near) the refrigerator. The glass of water that holds the temperature probe will buffer the swings in the temperature caused by the cycling of the compressor.

Hygrometer

The digital thermometer with cable probe does have merits, but it is my opinion that the *wireless indoor/outdoor thermo-hygrometer* described earlier in this chapter is best for monitoring the meat-aging refrigerator. However, if you think it would be more suitable for your application if the hygrometer were separate, there are numerous kinds of hygrometers listed on the Internet at various prices.

Refrigerator Fan

When meat is dry aged, one of the most important goals is to dry the surface slowly and uniformly. This drying produces a hard rind—normally about ¼ inch (about 7 mm) thick. The hard, dry rind seals the surface, blocking excessive moisture loss and providing a moisture-free surface that discourages the growth of mold and helps to kill bacteria and block the entry of bacteria into the raw meat. (Freshly slaughtered meat from healthy animals is naturally free of bacteria until its surface is contaminated during the butchering process.)

This slow and uniform drying is facilitated by a combination of a relative humidity ranging from 50 to 85 percent and *good air circulation*. The ideal relative humidity range is debated by dry-aging professionals. Some professionals feel that a tighter target range of about 70 to 80 percent should be maintained. My experience indicates that anywhere within the range of 50 to 85 percent produces a good result. Please be aware that the humidity will be high (about 85 percent) for the first two weeks or so. This initial high humidity is caused by the fact that moisture evaporates easily from the damp surface of fresh meat. However, when the hard rind develops on the meat, this rind will greatly hinder evaporation, and the humidity will fall. When it begins to fall, place a pan of water in the refrigerator to maintain a humidity level in the acceptable range. I use a large, rectangular Pyrex baking dish. Because the dish is rather wide and long, a large surface area of water is exposed to the air in the fridge. When the humidity falls beyond a certain point, the water in the Pyrex dish will automatically evaporate to replace it.

The ideal airflow speed inside the refrigerator is often said to be about 5 miles per hour (8 kph). To accomplish the desired airflow, all impediments to air circulation must be removed and at least one small fan must be used to force the circulation. I have found that using two small fans, rather than one fan, is more effective for achieving the desirable volume of critical air circulation.

If you are using a mini refrigerator (4 to 5 cubic feet—about 0.127 cubic meter) with a tiny ice cube chamber near the top of the compartment, the following actions should result in unimpeded air circulation:

- If glass shelves are being used, replace them with wire shelves.
- There will normally be a drip tray under the ice cube chamber. (Some mini refrigerators have neither an ice cube chamber nor a drip tray.) This drip tray will likely have raised slots that may appear to permit the free flow of air, *but they do not! Remove this drip tray during the dry-aging session and replace it when you are manually defrosting the refrigerator between dry-aging sessions. The drip tray for my refrigerator is shown in a photo near the beginning of this chapter. This drip tray is located immediately below the frost-covered freezing compartment.*

The fan. The following type of fan will provide excellent air circulation for a mini refrigerator, and installation is not difficult—it is a "plug-and-play" operation: Mini USB Powered Desktop Cooling Fan. This tiny fan is designed to set on a table or desk and plug into a computer's USB socket (*USB* means "*Universal Serial Bus*"). (Of course,

Two small desk fans were required to provide good air circulation. This fan is permanently mounted (with duct tape) in one of the door shelves.

the intended purpose of a desktop cooling fan is to keep comfortable a person working at a desk—and probably using a computer—or commonly to cool the computer itself. However, it works perfectly to provide the required air circulation for a mini refrigerator being used as a dry-aging chamber.)

Such a fan with about a 4-inch (10 cm) blade will do the job, but you may find, as I did, that two fans are required to get excellent air circulation. Prices vary. You will also need a 5V power adapter so that the fan (or fans) can connect to the 120V wall socket instead of a computer USB socket. The power adapter can likely be purchased for $5 or less, but some desktop cooling fans come with the 5V power adapter. (One of my desktop cooling fans was purchased at a hardware store for about $12, and it included a power adapter.)

Installation of the fan is easy:

1. Place the fan near the top or bottom of the refrigerator compartment and point it toward the meat. Obviously, it must be placed on a wire shelf if it is near the top of the fridge. (I put a second fan in one of the door shelves inside the refrigerator.)
2. Feed the USB cable to the outside of the refrigerator. (The USB cable diameter is small, so the rubber door gasket will close snugly over the cord.)
3. Plug the USB cable into the 5V power adapter and then plug the power adapter into the wall socket. (The power adapter is not necessary if there is an open USB socket on a nearby computer.)

CUTTING BOARD

It is difficult and awkward to prepare large cuts of meat for dry aging without a cutting board. If you do not have one, you might consider buying a modern plastic type that measures at least 12 x 18 inches (30 x 45 cm). Wooden cutting boards are porous and difficult to clean, so they are good breeding grounds for germs, bacteria, and mold spores—all of which need to be scrupulously avoided when dry aging. A stiff scrub brush, used with dish detergent and hot water, is very effective for cleaning your cutting board. Use a bleach-and-water solution and a fresh water rinse to remove most stains and to sterilize the board. About 1 teaspoon (5 ml) of common laundry bleach to 1 quart (1 L) of water works well.

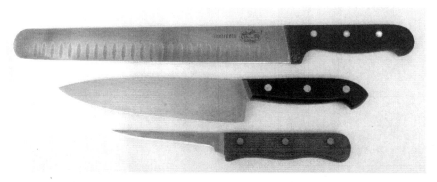

From top to bottom: a slicing knife, a general-purpose knife, and a boning knife.

KNIVES

Trimming and cutting meat is a major part of dry aging, but only about three kinds of knives are required. They should be of the proper shape and length to do the job at hand. If they are always kept sharp and used properly, your work will proceed efficiently and safely. They need not be expensive; good-quality used knives in good condition are an excellent choice. They need only be sharpened.

Knives with plain edges are better than those with serrated cutting edges. Serrated edges tend to saw food, rather than cut it cleanly. Furthermore, serrated blades are difficult or impossible to sharpen.

Knives should never be washed in a dishwasher, especially knives that have wooden handles. The very hot water used for washing in a dishwasher, and the high heat used for drying, will gradually damage the wood by removing its natural oils. The loss of natural oils and the resultant cracking of the wood will cause the handle rivets to loosen.

The kind of steel used to make a knife blade is not very important; it is mostly a matter of personal preference.

Carbon steel is the choice of many because it holds its edge fairly well and is easy to sharpen. One disadvantage is that the blade will tarnish, but most of the tarnish can be removed with steel wool. Another minor negative point is that a carbon-steel blade may impart a me-tallic taste and odor to acidic foods such as tomatoes, onions, and citrus fruits.

Stainless steel used to make high-quality knives is not the same kind of stainless steel used to make your mixing bowls or your rust-proof mailbox. *Stainless steel* is a general term for many different al-loys. Your mixing bowls are probably made with 18 percent chromium and 8 percent nickel. An alloy used to make high-quality stainless steel knives might contain small amounts of molybdenum, vanadium, manganese, and carbon in addition to the chromium and nickel. In other words, *stainless steel* is not an exact term, but a high-quality stain-less steel knife will be made of an alloy that will hold its edge for a long time. This is good, of course. The other side of the coin is that a knife that holds its edge well, such as a high-quality stainless-steel knife, will be difficult to sharpen once the edge is dull.

High-carbon stainless-steel knives are among the most expensive. The steel used in these knives has the rust- and stain-resistant proper-ties of ordinary stainless-steel knives, but they sharpen as easily as the carbon-steel knives. Of course, because they are easy to sharpen, they do not hold their edge as well as the common stainless-steel knives.

Boning Knife

The term *boning knife* may be a slight misnomer. With its slender blade and blade length of 6 inches (15 cm) or less, it is a very handy knife for boning meat, but it may be used more often to trim meat. For ex-ample, the first step in preparing a cut of meat for dry aging is to trim the meat to improve the appearance. This is also the knife of choice for removing the hard rind (crust) from the surface of the meat after the dry aging has been completed. The boning knife is one of the es-sential knives for dry aging.

Slicing Knife

A slicing knife is another essential knife. Large subprimal cuts of quality beef are possibly the most common dry-aged items, and these large hunks of meat often need to be sliced into steaks after the dry aging is finished. It is easy to slice steaks if you use a straight knife with a blade at least 12 inches (30 cm) long; longer is better. In fact, a slicing knife is helpful to slice many other items: leg of lamb and goose breast, for example.

General-Purpose Knife

A general-purpose knife has many meat preparation applications. Depending on the style, such a knife is commonly known as a *butcher knife, chef's knife,* or *French knife.* The length of a general-purpose knife is a personal preference.

In recent years, the Japanese *santoku* knives are becoming popular in the United States, and they are frequently manufactured in this country. The meaning of *santoku* is "three virtues" or "three uses"; the knife is considered by the Japanese to be useful for slicing, dicing, and mincing. Typically, a *santoku* blade is 5 to 8 inches long (13–20 cm) and is shaped somewhat like a French knife.

A good quality knife sharpener for home use, an eight-inch (20 cm) Carborundum whetstone, and a butcher's steel.

KNIFE SHARPENER

Electric knife sharpeners have improved greatly over the years, and good sharpeners are available in the $40 to $60 price range. If they are used carefully, they do a fast and efficient job of keeping your knives in a like-new condition. It is recommended, however, that the knives be honed briefly with a whetstone or butcher's steel after using the electric knife sharpener. The brief honing will remove the burrs and edge curl caused by the knife sharpener. (*See the following section.*)

Whetstone and Butcher's Steel

You should use a whetstone to keep your knives sharp. It can be used to sharpen your knives from start to finish, or it can be used to touch up the knives between major sharpening sessions with an electric sharpener. A Carborundum whetstone is inexpensive, and it is easily found at a culinary supply or hardware store. I suggest that you buy one at least 8 inches (20 cm) long and 2 inches (5 cm) wide. A laminated stone that is coarse on one side and fine on the other is convenient. If a thin stream of water is allowed to fall on the stone while knives are being sharpened, the stone's surface will not become clogged with metallic dust. The kitchen sink is the best place to sharpen knives. Use a dishpan (or the like) turned upside down as a platform for the stone, and while the blade is being honed, allow a tiny stream of water to fall on the whetstone to wash away the metallic dust.

A butcher's steel (also called *knife steel* or *sharpening steel*) looks something like a long rat-tail file. Most sharpening steels will not remove metal from the knife blade, but they will straighten the edge curl that develops when a knife is used or when it is sharpened with an electric knife sharpener. The butcher's steel is not essential equipment, but frequent use of one will prolong the sharpness of the blade. The longer the butcher's steel, the easier it is to use—especially for knives with long blades. Ceramic rod is also used to make this knife-honing tool. Ceramic works equally well.

WEIGHT SCALES

A weight scale is not essential for dry-aging operations, but it is very useful. Most meat-aging practitioners want to know the weight of the subprimal cut at the start of the session and at the end. This allows them to calculate moisture loss. Also, weighing the meat after trimming off the hard, inedible, rind helps to calculate the waste caused by dry aging.

An inexpensive food scale that will weigh up to about 11 pounds of meat (about 5 kg) will do the job in most cases. But if you intend to use very large subprimal cuts, a scale that will weigh up to about 22 pounds (10 kg) would be required. A highly accurate scale is not required by the average dry-aging hobbyist; a scale that provides consistent readings for the same object is more important.

CHAPTER 3

Health Matters

The practice of dry aging food may cause concern because it appears to have the potential to cause illness. I hope that it will be reassuring for me to mention that in all of the years I have done meat processing (including making sausage, smoking food, and dry-aging meat), not once has a product spoiled during processing, and not once has a product caused food poisoning or any other health-related problem. If safe food-handling guidelines are practiced, dry aging poses no more of a health risk than common cooking.

THE PROBLEM

In this age, the average adult in any modern country is aware of germs and the most common diseases related to food. We are aware that sanitation helps to prevent the spread of disease, and we know that refrigeration retards spoilage.

The meat-aging hobbyist, however, needs to have a bit more knowledge about such matters than the average person does. This is because dry aging meat involves subjecting food to conditions that come close to the limits of safe food handling. For example, although the aging meat is held within a temperature range that discourages spoilage (34–38°F, or 1–3°C), the meat is held under refrigeration for an exceedingly long time. And this exceedingly long time provides greater opportunity for spoilage and the proliferation of harmful microbes. Special precautions need to be taken to prevent this.

In order to dry age meat so that it is safe for human consumption, we must know how to prevent the growth of microbes that cause illness. One of the most important things to know is that harmful microbes do not normally exist *inside* the flesh of healthy livestock or healthy wild game. However, the *surface* of the meat will usually become contaminated as soon as the animal is slaughtered, skinned, and butchered. The microbes that cause the contamination are present on any unsterilized tools and equipment used in this process. Also, hide, fur, skin, and feathers are notorious for harboring malicious microbes. And as soon as the nasty critters contact the surface of the moist and nourishing raw meat, they begin to multiply. When we dry age the meat, it is imperative that we do everything possible to prevent the proliferation of the microbes, prevent them from entering the flesh, and destroy the ones that are on the surface. The changes going on *inside* the hunk of meat that are caused by the uncontrolled muscle enzymes (discussed in chapter 5) are desirable because flavor and tenderness are improved by the changes they engender. However, bacterial activity on the *surface* of the meat is dangerous and disgusting; some of the bacteria feasting on the slaughtered animal flesh are also capable of feasting on the flesh of a living human being that digests them.

THE STEPS TO TAKE

Eating food always involves risk. For example, there are many causes of food poisoning, and unknowingly contracting it is always a possibility. All of us have heard of salmonella, *E. coli* 0157, and other food-related illness. Eating dry-aged meat that has been stored, unwrapped, in a refrigerator for six weeks or more sounds scary to most people. But the chances of becoming ill by eating properly processed dry-aged meat is less than the chance of getting sick by eating common restaurant fare.

Even though the possibility of getting sick by eating dry-aged meat is remote, the following guidelines should minimize this possibility.

Pay Attention to the Smell, Touch, and Appearance

Meat that has been properly dry aged will not be spoiled. However, unplanned, unexpected, unimagined, and even unknown events can occur and cause improper aging. If it smells like it is rotten, it is rotten and must be discarded even if you do not have a clue as to what went wrong. Properly dry-aged meat should never smell foul. Furthermore, if the touch is slimy, or if it is covered by mold, throw it away and then try to figure out what went wrong.

How many times have I had to discard spoiled dry-aged meat? Not even one time. Never. But it may happen sometime in the future. An electric power failure could cause the problem. Starting out with improperly stored or tainted meat could be the reason. Some event that resulted in a relative humidity environment of over 85 percent for a lengthy period could cause fungal proliferation.

Use a Clean, Dedicated, Refrigerator

If the refrigerator is used only for dry aging, contamination by the bacteria and fungi that are carried by almost all natural food products is minimized. This is why the refrigerator should be dedicated solely to the dry aging of meat.

The battle against microbes is never-ending. *At the beginning of every dry-aging session, the refrigerator should be sanitized. Chapter 4 gives step-by-step instructions to sanitize the refrigerator quickly, easily, and effectively. This is important.*

Revere the Rind

Because the hunk of meat is unwrapped and exposed to air in the chamber of the refrigerator for many days or weeks, most of the moisture *on* the meat, and some of the moisture *in* it, will evaporate. This evaporation has both good and bad consequences, but the most important point is that the evaporation, especially the evaporation on the surface of the meat, prevents it from spoiling. *Because spoilage is prevented by evaporation of surface moisture, dry aging of meat is possible.*

How does this evaporation on the surface of the meat prevent the meat from rotting? The reason is that the bacteria on the surface of the meat that can cause rotting are living organisms, and they require moisture to survive and reproduce. The cold temperature inside the refrigerator has already discouraged growth, and depriving them of moisture presents them with a double whammy that ensures their demise. As previously mentioned, meat from healthy animals does not normally contain microbes within the muscle tissue, so the dehydration of the first few millimeters (about ¼ inch) of the surface spells death for any microbes that may be there. The same can be said for fungal spores. This layer of hard, dry surface is called the *rind* or *crust*.

You may find instructions on the Internet, or elsewhere, to wrap the meat in cheesecloth while it is being aged. I have never seen or heard a good and believable reason for this, and professional meat agers never wrap with cheesecloth; consequently, I don't recommend it. The main reason I advise against the practice is that it might interfere with the all-important formation of the rind.

CHAPTER 4

Controlling Refrigerator Bacteria, Mold, and Odors

Controlling bacteria, mold, and odors in the refrigerator is a very important part of dry aging. These three items can present a health hazard or make the finished product look, taste, or smell repulsive. Good sanitation minimizes bacteria, mold, and odors. Consequently, controlling bacteria, mold, and odors with good sanitation is just as important as controlling temperature and humidity.

- Mold and bacteria proliferation are inhibited by the 34 to 38°F (1–3°C) temperature that is maintained in a dry-aging environment.
- Ensuring that relative humidity does not exceed 85 percent lessens the opportunity for mold and bacteria to thrive; mold and bacteria require more moisture than that provided by 85 percent relative humidity.
- Even in a dedicated refrigerator used only for dry aging, the spoilage of food smudges and debris remaining on the inside surface of an unclean refrigerator interior can taint the meat being processed. *A higher level of sanitation is required for a dedicated dry-aging refrigerator than for a common household refrigerator.*

Controlling temperature and humidity is invariably recognized to be important by serious meat-aging hobbyists, but the importance of a clean refrigerator is often overlooked. For example, hobbyists may be adamant about reducing the spread of contamination by using plastic cutting boards—rather than wooden ones—and they might insist that the cutting boards be scrubbed and disinfected frequently. Nevertheless, they might not realize that putting meat into an unclean dry-aging refrigerator is akin to putting it on a dirty cutting board or into a dirty container. They might have to confess that they have never seriously cleaned their refrigerator since the appliance store delivered it to their house.

SANITIZING THE DRY-AGING REFRIGERATOR

The dry-aging process requires meat to remain in the refrigerator about 7 to 60 days, or longer, at temperatures between 34 and 38°F (1–3°C) and at a relative humidity between 50 and 85 percent. Meat held under these conditions can certainly be free of harmful bacteria, mold, and bad odors if attention is paid to the various factors that cause these problems. Proper sanitation helps to prevent these three problems and thus contributes to making the dry-aging session a success.

The refrigerator sanitation procedure given below may seem excessive, but I strongly recommend that you adopt it as described here—it will help ensure the safety of your food, and might prevent you from having to throw a $150 hunk of rib eye in the garbage.

Sanitation Steps That Should Be Taken Before Every Dry-Aging Session

Note: *The cleaning agents recommended below, used as recommended, will result in very effective, safe, and economical sanitation of the refrigerator. The agents will also accomplish the sanitation process without leaving odors or residues that will taint or contaminate the meat being processed. Do not substitute manufactured cleaning liquids, spray cleaners, or the like.*

1. Unplug the refrigerator and the portable electric fan(s) being used for air circulation. (If these appliances are not

disconnected, the water solutions used for cleaning could cause a short circuit, which might result in a fire, result in damage to the refrigerator or fan(s), or result in a harmful or fatal electric shock.) After cleaning the refrigerator, allow adequate time for the refrigerator and fan(s) to dry thoroughly before connecting them to electricity again.

2. If necessary, defrost the refrigerator.

3. Remove all items from the shelves. (Since this is a refrigerator dedicated to dry aging, it should not be used for food storage between dry-aging sessions: Common grocery items can introduce unwanted bacteria and mold spores, and they may leave an odor residue that taints the next dry-age batch.)

4. To a bucketful of hot water, or to a sink containing about a bucketful of hot water, add 3 tablespoons (45 ml) of dish detergent. Mix well.

5. Remove *everything* from the refrigerator. This includes all of the shelves and the air-circulating fan(s). There should be no produce drawers or ice cube trays in this dedicated dry-aging refrigerator because they serve no useful purpose. In fact, these unused items serve only to increase the length of time required to sanitize the refrigerator.

6. Wash the removed refrigerator shelves thoroughly with a freshly laundered cloth or with disposable paper towels dipped in the hot, soapy water. Wipe the outside surface of the portable electric fan(s).

7. Don rubber gloves. Put 1 gallon (4 L) of hot water in a bucket. Add 1 tablespoon (15 ml) of chlorine bleach (common laundry bleach) to make a sanitizing solution. Mix the bleach into the water with a gloved hand.

8. Dip all of the refrigerator chamber parts, except the fan(s), in the water-and-bleach solution, then rinse them in fresh water. If they are too large to dip and rinse, wipe the parts with paper towels or with a freshly laundered cloth that has been dipped in the water-and-bleach solution, and then wipe with fresh water. The outside surface of the fan(s) should be wiped in the same way. Set everything aside on a clean surface to air-dry.

9. Mix about 1 cup (240 ml) of white vinegar with 1 cup (240 ml) of warm water in a container. Dip a fresh cleaning cloth in the solution and wring it so it is wet but not dripping. Wipe down the entire refrigerator, inside first, and then outside, including the handles—do not forget to wipe the inside of the refrigerator door. Use a toothbrush to get into any creases or depressions.

10. Sprinkle a little baking soda on stubborn stains or stuck-on food. Then scrub these away using a cloth or toothbrush dipped in the 50–50 vinegar-and-water mixture. (The baking soda powder acts as a gentle abrasive.)

11. Dip a fresh cloth into the bleach-and-water solution. Wring it well and wipe down the entire refrigerator, inside first, and then outside, including the handles—do not forget to wipe the inside of the refrigerator door and the rubber door gasket with the solution. Finally, use a clean cloth to wipe down all of these surfaces with fresh water. Let the fridge air-dry. Reconnect the power cord to the refrigerator. If necessary, reset the temperature-control dial.

Wash your hands thoroughly, and then replace the shelves and other items. The refrigerator is now ready for the next meat-aging session.

Commercial and Amateur Dry Aging of Various Meats

This chapter will touch upon some of the most significant points regarding the dry-aging process as it is applied to the meat of various animals and fowl. It will also compare commercial and amateur dry aging. Wet aging will also be discussed and compared with dry aging. In short, this chapter will touch on many important dry-aging topics, and later chapters will address specific issues regarding specific kinds of meats. If you are looking for some general or technical information on the subject of dry aging, look it up in the index at the back of this book. The index will often to guide you to a page located here in chapter 5.

Important Point: Chapter 12 is one of the shortest chapters in the book, but it is also one of the most important. Chapter 12 will show you, step by step, how to dry age *any kind of meat.* It will tell you what to do and when to do it. It will tell you what to measure and when, where, and how to measure it. It will tell you what decisions you must make and explain the criteria for making them. Check out chapter 12 when you are ready to begin dry aging.

THE COMMERCIAL DRY AGING OF BEEF

As mentioned in chapter 1, dry aging of meat has been practiced for countless years by hunters of big game, small game, and wild fowl. It is unclear how long *commercial* dry aging of meat has been practiced, but even as recently as 100 years ago it was not economically significant. It was not until the 1950s that the producers of beef realized that hanging the carcass under controlled conditions for a limited time would be profitable. Until that time, most producers did not realize that it would result in a product that would increase income enough to justify the extra effort and expense.

Below, a summary of some of the information provided in the chapter 1 introduction will be presented again order give a complete summary of the modern dry aging of beef, the most famous of dry-aged meat.

Initially, in the 1950s, the practice of dry aging the beef carcass spread rapidly in the United States and other developed countries in the world. However, new meat packaging technology developed in the early 1960s not only brought a halt to the rapid spread of this practice, it almost ended commercial dry aging of beef.

The new technology that stifled the practice of dry aging beef was the development of heavy-duty plastic bags for meatpacking, and the coinciding development of vacuum packing. Vacuum packing beef in its own juices, together with the "aging time" ("aging time" for the vacuum-packed beef was largely nothing more than the shipping time), resulted in increased tenderness, and this increased tenderness was obtained at very little cost. The cost of wet aging was essentially limited to the cost of the following: heavy-duty, vacuum-sealable plastic bags; the depreciation of the cost of vacuum-packing equipment; and the minor labor cost for the vacuum packing.

Dry aging, on the other hand, could result in an appealing nutty, cheesy, or meaty flavor and aroma; wet aging could not. Additionally, dry aging could bring about increased juiciness and tenderness; wet aging could do this to some extent, but dry aging could do it better. These important and desirable results of dry aging any kind of meat are pointed out on the first page of the first chapter of this book.

However, this enhanced appeal of the professionally processed dry-aged beef came at a high cost: Dry aging causes a significant moisture loss, and moisture loss translates directly into weight loss. The drying effect also causes the formation of a hard, inedible rind on the surface of the meat that must be trimmed off and discarded. This resulting loss of weight caused by moisture loss and rind formation is considerable, and the potential loss of profit must be recovered when the meat is sold. But this is not all: Dry aging requires greatly extended storage time in sophisticated and expensive storage areas with concurrent labor costs. This loss of weight, coupled with the high processing costs, results in a significantly higher retail price.

THE COMMERCIAL AND AMATEUR DRY AGING OF NON-BEEF MEATS

In this book, we will explore the commercial and amateur dry aging of other meats, too, such as venison, duck, goose, lamb, mutton, and goat. The meat of any animal or bird can be dry aged. One rule of thumb is that the dry-aging time must be shortened as the percentage of unsaturated fat increases. The main reason is that unsaturated fat becomes increasingly rancid the longer it is exposed to oxygen.

Why is there no chapter in this book for dry aging birds like chicken and domesticated turkey? Well, these birds have high percentage of unsaturated fat, and they are harvested when they are young and tender. The high percentage of unsaturated fat means that they cannot be dry aged long enough to make a significant difference in flavor, and the fact that they are young and tender means that the tenderization provided by dry aging is not required. For these reasons, the dry aging of chicken and turkey is not considered worth the effort by most dry-aging enthusiasts. Also, the insignificant change produced by the dry aging of these birds means that few people are willing to pay the very significant increase in the retail price for a professionally dry-aged chicken or turkey. (In the third paragraph of chapter 8, *Dry-Aged Duck*, there is an interesting comparison of dry-aged duck and dry-aged chicken.)

The wild pheasant is a popular game bird with light-colored breast meat like the chicken and the turkey (however, the breast meat of a pheasant is usually described as pink, rather than white). Most people consider it an exotic meat. It is almost a certainty that someone has dry aged a pheasant, but I can find no record of it. I assume that anyone who tried it would likely have concluded that it was not worth the effort. The limited benefits, if any, would not likely justify the effort required to dry age the bird. Neither flavor enhancement nor tenderization would be likely because the period of dry aging would be limited by the high percent of unsaturated fat. Nevertheless, if you have access to pheasant, and if you are adventurous, you might want to try it.

Many other meats benefit from dry aging, however. Even meat from the common pig, from feral pigs, or from wild boar can be dry aged. Still, as mentioned above, it would be generally agreed that the dry-aging time must be shorter than that for beef because the percent of unsaturated fat is higher. Unfortunately, as noted, when the dry-aging time is shorter, there is less chance for flavor development. Furthermore, many people are quite satisfied with the unique and rich flavors of domesticated and wild pig meats, and they do not want the dry-aged flavor to be superimposed on it. Added to that is the fact the tenderizing effect is not necessary for the common meat-market pork because it comes from young and tender juvenile swine. For all these reasons, *there is little interest in dry-aging domesticated pork because the process isn't necessary to improve flavor or tenderness. If feral pork or wild boar is dry aged, it is usually done solely to improve tenderness.*

Having said that, I would like to point out that I recently read an Internet article written in May 2014 by a man named Chef Schneller who teaches at The Culinary Institute of America, Hyde Park Campus, in New York. He reported dry aging large cuts of pork with the skin and fat intact for 30 days and for 60 days. He concluded: "The flavor was certainly richer and full with slight undertones of that same distinct flavor that is dry aged beef. The older one started to get a little strong or musty in flavor. The result, in general, was that pork can be dry aged to improve taste." (I am sure that when he used the term *older one*, he was referring to the large cut of pork that was aged 60 days.)

I am not surprised that he claimed success in dry aging pork, because the percent of unsaturated fat in pork is between that of beef and lamb. However, the change of taste he equates with improvement might not be considered an improvement by everyone. (But it might be considered an improvement by you or me.) Nevertheless, the report of his tests has caught my attention, and I will definitely dry age a hunk of pork in the near future. However, when I age it the first time, there is no possibility that I will age it for 60 days. For my first dry-aging test on pork, about 30 days sounds good to me. Chef Schneller said that the pork he aged for 60 days tasted rancid; I believe him, and I do not like rancid meat, so I will go for the 30 days.

DRY AGING THE MEAT AT HOME

It is very unlikely that new technology or improved processing equipment will reduce the cost of dry aging meat to the point that it can meaningfully compete with the wet-aged variety. However, a meat-processing hobbyist can make dry-aged meats at home, and make them at a very affordable cost. It will not be necessary to mortgage the house in order to treat your family and friends to a dry-aged steak dinner. Furthermore, these meats will match or exceed the quality of dry-aged meats being offered on the retail market. If you're thinking about adopting this hobby, you may wish to consider another important point: The dry aging of meat is not limited to beef. Lamb, goose, duck, goat, pork, and wild game meat can be dry aged. Even photographs of dry-aged kangaroo appear on the Internet.

CHANGES CAUSED BY DRY AGING

Dry aging of meat causes significant changes in the meat. If the dry aging is practiced with a reasonable amount of care, the results will be consistent, predictable, healthy, and—normally—desirable: The dry-aged meat will usually be more tender and juicy, and it will usually have an enhanced flavor.

Wine and cheese benefit from aging, and many kinds of meat can, too. Aging is a slow chemical change. With proper aging, most meats will become more tender and flavorful. The aging of meat is an easy, safe, understandable, rewarding, and predictable process.

Harold McGee, the author of *On Food and Cooking* and a worldwide authority on food science, has described the changes that take place when meat is dry aged under the proper conditions. (His book is used widely in food science courses at many universities, and it has won numerous awards.) The following descriptions of those changes are based on his explanations, and those of other respected experts in food science and dry aging.

Flavor Changes

The aging of meat is mainly the work of muscle enzymes. (Enzymes are complex proteins.) The scientific word is *proteolysis*, or breakdown of muscle proteins. After an animal is slaughtered, the muscle enzymes are no longer controlled, and they begin to attack other cells. They convert large, bland-tasting molecules into tasty fragments. For example, proteins are changed to delicious amino acids (there are 20 amino acids, and they produce many kinds of taste sensations): Glycogen is changed into glucose, a kind of sugar; ATP (called an energy currency) is transformed into a tasty compound called IMP, or inosinic acid (which is used by the food industry as a flavor enhancer).

The changes mentioned in the sleep-inducing paragraph above are only some of flavor-affecting changes taking place while meat is dry aging. Most of us do not yearn for more detail than this, but those who want even more technical information can find it in books on food science. You might wish to start with the above-mentioned book by Harold McGee.

Improved Tenderness and Juiciness

The same rampant enzyme activity that causes improved flavor also causes the meat of the slaughtered animal to become more tender. (This enzyme activity is described above in the section titled *Flavor Changes.*) In this case, however, the enzymes called *calpains* and *cathepsins* weaken and break apart various proteins, filaments, supporting molecules, and connective tissue, as well as performing other violent and difficult-to-comprehend tenderizing activities.

The result of the rampant enzyme activity is twofold: Not only does the meat become tenderized and succulent because its collagen is gelatinized, but it becomes juicier because the weakened connective tissue causes it to shrink less during cooking. When the meat shrinks less, less moisture is squeezed out.

Flavor Concentration During Aging

Dry-aged meat can lose over 20 percent of its initial volume due to evaporation of some of the water content. Obviously, this will result in a more concentrated and a more intense flavor.

REFRIGERATOR TEMPERATURE AND HUMIDITY

No matter what kind of meat is being dry aged, the desirable temperature and humidity conditions are the same. The average temperature of the dry-aging compartment (refrigerator) should be maintained within a range of about 34 to 38°F (1–3°C). Of course, when the door of the refrigerator is opened, the temperature will usually climb, but this presents no problem as long as the temperature goes back to the desired range within a reasonable time after the door is closed.

A moderate humidity range is required in the aging chamber. However, the definition of *moderate* is not the same among all the experts. All agree that the range should be low enough to discourage fungal growth, but high enough to cause the meat to lose moisture gradually. Depending on the opinion of the dry-aging expert being consulted, the recommended average humidity *range* of the dry-aging chamber is as narrow as 50 to 75 percent, and as wide as 50 to 85 percent.

My experience indicates that the acceptable relative humidity has a wide range. No matter what time of year I am dry aging meat, I am able to maintain a relative humidity of no lower than 52 percent and no higher than 82 percent without using sophisticated humidity-controlling equipment (the average is probably around 75 percent). This range has always produced good results. I have never experienced any humidity-related problems such as excessive drying or objectionable mold formation.

I have found, by the way, that I need not be concerned about excessive drying because the meat surface begins to dry and harden immediately, and this drying and hardening of the surface increasingly reduces the escape of moisture. After about two weeks of dry aging, the moisture-proof rind has formed perfectly on the surface of the meat. This rind essentially blocks additional drying and protects against mold formation. (I know that no noticeable additional drying takes place because I found that the weight of the meat did not decrease significantly after the initial two weeks.) Consequently, it is my opinion that—because of the rapid rind formation—the tight control of relative humidity is of minor importance.

A brown Pyrex-glass water tray for humidity stabilization is placed in the bottom of the dry aging refrigerator. The two strips of wood directly under the tray function to lift the tray and allow the door to close.

The only thing that I do to help maintain an acceptable relative humidity range is to place a rectangular Pyrex baking dish in the refrigerator and keep it full of water. The amount and depth of the water are not important because only the area of the exposed water surface will affect the relative humidity. If the Pyrex dish is placed in the bottom of the refrigerator, it also functions as a drip tray to catch the occasional drops of blood from the meat. There will be no problems caused by the water being tainted by blood, although you can change the water at will to maintain a sanitary and tidy appearance. If you do so, it is best to use water that is very near the same temperature as the dirty water in the dish. If the freshwater temperature is about the same as that of the bloodstained water, there will not be an unwelcome change in the refrigerator temperature.

Water evaporating from this dish replaces the moisture that has been solidified into frost by the evaporator coils in the manual-defrost refrigerator. I have read about some people who were very concerned about keeping the relative humidity controlled more tightly, so they installed a room humidifier and an electrical humidity controller in their refrigerator; the controller turns the humidifier off and on. I was going to do a similar installation if I found it to be necessary, but I have used the Pyrex dish for a long time now, and I am satisfied with it: In my opinion, a room humidifier and an electrical humidity controller is a waste of money and refrigerator space.

As indicated in chapter 2, in the section *Refrigerator-Related Equipment,* I believe that a wireless digital electronic thermo-hygrometer is the best instrument for monitoring both the internal temperature *and* the internal relative humidity of the dry-aging refrigerator. Keep in mind that this device will show the changes in temperature and relative humidity almost instantaneously. Here are some examples: If the refrigerator automatically turns on and the refrigerant begins to flow in the evaporator coils, the thermometer will show a quickly falling temperature; the hygrometer will show a rather quickly rising relative humidity. (When air cools, it contracts and loses volume; this causes the percent of moisture in the air to increase.)

If you want to consider an alternative to the wireless digital electronic thermo-hygrometer, there are additional suggestions for monitoring devices described in chapter 2.

AGING TIME

When meat is being aged, remember to turn it over occasionally so that all surfaces are equally exposed to airflow. During the first few days, it would be best to turn the meat over daily, then every other day for the next few days. After about 10 days, turning the meat over once every 3 days is sufficient.

There are no hard-and-fast rules for the number of days to age meat. In order to decide on that number, several things must be considered.

The first thing to consider is the kind of meat. Some meats tolerate dry aging better than others do. The main factor that limits the dry-aging time for a certain kind of meat is its amount of unsaturated fat. (Unsaturated fat, by the way, is usually fluid at room temperature.) The amount of unsaturated fat in fish and chicken is great. Beef, on the other hand, has more saturated fat than any other commonly eaten meat. When unsaturated fat is exposed to the air, as it is when it's dry aged, the fat absorbs oxygen and develops a rancid taste. Consequently, fish and chicken will become rancid much more quickly than beef. Beef tolerates dry aging better than all the commonly eaten meats do, so it can be dry aged longer. Suggested dry-aging times for the meats featured in this book are discussed in their respective chapters. The suggested dry-aging time for duck, for example, is discussed in chapter 8. (For discussion of the dry-aging time for pork and chicken, please see chapter 5.)

The diet of the animal may affect the aging time. For example, meat from animals such as beef cattle that have had a grass diet cannot be dry aged as long as cattle that have been fed on grain. This is because the grain-fed cattle's meat has a blander flavor that is more compatible with the distinct flavor imparted by the dry-aging process.

The overall size of the object being dry aged is also a factor because the distinct dry-age flavor is imparted most strongly on the surface. Consequently, primal cuts of a specific large cut of thick meat are dry aged longer than the smaller and thinner subprimal cuts, and large domesticated ducks are aged longer than the smaller wild ducks.

MORE VARIETIES OF MEAT TO DRY AGE

The chapters that follow deal with the dry aging of many types of meat, and suggestions are given for the length of time to dry age them. Special dry-aging techniques for those meat varieties are suggested. Please keep in mind, however, that personal preference is always the most important consideration when you're considering dry-aging time.

STORING DRY-AGED MEAT

When the meat has been dry aged long enough to suit your taste, it should be refrigerated and then consumed as soon as possible. If it cannot be cooked and eaten within about three days, it should be frozen. Freezing dry-aged meat will halt the aging process and prevent it from spoiling, but freezing should not done as a matter of course and it should not be done repeatedly; the product will deteriorate in quality every time it is frozen and thawed.

If the finished product will be frozen, it must be wrapped in airtight packaging or vacuum packed. The sooner it is thawed and eaten, the better it will taste. Long-term freezing can cause rancidity. Dry-aged meat should not be thawed at room temperature because microorganisms can grow exponentially at temperatures above 41°F (5°C).

CHAPTER 6

Dry-Aged Beef

ABOUT DRY-AGED BEEF

Important Point: This chapter provides information about dry-aged beef. Chapter 12 will show you, step by step, how to dry age beef or *any other kind of meat.*

Beef is, by far, the most commonly dry-aged meat. One reason for this is that beef fat is the most highly saturated meat fat, which means it does not absorb oxygen and become rancid as quickly as other meats. This allows beef to be dry aged longer and thus become more tender and flavorful than other meats. Some restaurants serve steaks that have been aged 35, 42, or even more than 56 days. Saison, a restaurant in San Francisco, regularly serves 90-day beefsteak. Eleven Madison Park in New York offers steak that has been dry aged 140 days! However, beef aged 90 to 140 days would be too funky for most people; too much of a good thing often becomes a bad thing.

Almost any large hunk of beef can be dry aged, but subprimal cuts (large hunks) of either prime or choice grades of steak meat are most often selected. (The definitions of *primal cut* and *subprimal cut* appear in chapter 2. Somewhat confusingly, the expression *prime grade* means "top grade" or "first grade.")

As mentioned in the previous chapter, commercial dry aging is expensive. This is due to the cost of the extra labor, the equipment, the special facilities, the loss of product weight, and the capital it ties up. Another factor that adds to the production cost is the tendency to use superior-quality steak meat in order to obtain a very high-quality product that will fetch a high price. Subprimal cuts of rib eye, sirloin, and New York strip are the most commonly used cuts, and many of the high-class steak restaurants that serve dry-aged steak demand prime grade, the most expensive grade of beef. Some restaurants go so far as to specialize in Angus beef or even the very famous *wagyu* beef. *Wagyu* is the name used for any of several breeds of beef cattle that originated in Japan. The meats from all of these breeds are genetically predisposed to intense marbling. (You might be interested to know that in the Japanese language, *wa* means "Japanese" and *gyu* means "beef.")

Other cuts of beef are also dry aged; DeBragga & Spitler, a meat supply company in New York, offers dry-aged filet mignon, rib eye, T-bone, cowboy rib eye steak, and New York strip steaks. They also sell dry-aged Angus beef, *wagyu* beef, and standing rib roasts.

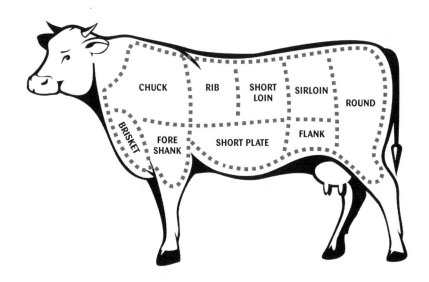

Beef cuts.

SELECTING A CUT OF BEEF

The first step in selecting a cut of beef for dry aging is finding a supplier that will provide you with the cut you need. You are more likely to get what you need at a privately owned butcher shop than at a big-box store or supermarket. Below are the points that should be considered when selecting a cut of beef for dry aging. (See color photos following page 56.)

- It is best if the cut is large; usually subprimal cuts (large, thick hunks) are selected. The reason for this is that the process of dry aging will form an inedible hard rind on the outside surfaces that are not covered by fat cap or bone. This rind is about ¼ inch (7 mm) thick, and it must be trimmed off and discarded. (Rather than discarding this rind, some people boil it and use it as dog food or boil it to make beef stock.) If the cut of meat is large and thick, and if most of the red meat is covered by fat cap and surface bone, the discarded rind will be a small percent of the total. If the cut of meat is small and thin, and a large area of red meat is exposed, however, there will be very little edible meat left after the rind is trimmed. (Another way of saying this is: *The lower the ratio of the surface area to the volume of the meat, the greater the amount of edible meat.*) Meat that has been cut into steaks, for example, should *never* be dry aged: Most, if not all of each steak would be converted into inedible rind.
- In most cases, beef is dry aged to make fantastically tender and delicious steaks, but beef is sometimes dry aged to make superb main-course entrées such as roast beef. Logically, if steak is the goal, a *subprimal* cut of beef that is commonly used for steak should be considered, and the *subprimal* cuts of rib eye, sirloin, and New York strip are the most common. These cuts come from areas of the bovine body that are exercised very little and are, therefore, tender.
- It is best if the subprimal cut has fat and bone on the outside surface. This prevents the edible red meat from becoming hard-and-dried rind that must be trimmed off and discarded. An area of fat on an outside surface is called a *fat cap*. The fat cap prevents rind development and, like the rind, prevents microbes from proliferating within the meat. Chine or any kind of bone on the surface also prevents rind development and, like the rind, prevents microbes from proliferating within the meat. A prime rib subprimal with a substantial fat cap and with the ribs and part of the chine

(backbone) intact is a perfect example of a good candidate for dry aging. However, most prime ribs that are distributed to supermarkets and retail butchers have much of the ribs and chine cut off.

- It may be that you like delicious steak, but you are on a tight budget. A cut of beef known as *top sirloin* might be a good choice. *Top sirloin* is an economical cut of meat from the subprimal *sirloin*, and when it is cut into steaks, they are logically called *top sirloin steaks*. *Sirloin steaks* are cut from a different and more tender part of the primal loin, and the price per pound for a large hunk of *sirloin* is considerably more than for *top sirloin*. Top sirloin has a partial fat cap that prevents rind development on about half of the surface. But, unfortunately, it does not have any bone on the remaining surface to reduce the formation of rind and protect the meat from infestation. Of course, when the dry aging is complete on the top sirloin subprimal, both the fat cap the rind are shaved off and discarded. There is no chine or other bone to cut off, so the area of rind that must be discarded is greater than for a sirloin subprimal. Nevertheless, the price per pound is significantly lower for the top sirloin, so it will usually be considerably more economical than the sirloin. Overall, if economy is important, this is an excellent choice. Of course, sirloin is a higher-quality steak meat, but top sirloin will become good steak meat after the tenderizing that comes from dry aging.

- A cut of beef called *plate* is part of the chest of a steer or heifer; it is located just behind the brisket. If the plate is cut into steaks, they are called *hanger steaks*. This cut of meat is very tender, and it is cheaper than most other steak meat, so it's worth consideration if economy is important. It is similar to flank steak in texture and flavor. It's best if the fat cap and rib bones are intact on the plate because they, too, prevent the edible red meat from drying and becoming inedible rind.

- Of all the cuts of beef that are suitable for dry aging, prime rib is one of easiest to obtain. It is often called prime rib *roast* because most people who buy such a large piece of meat intend to roast it. Being easy to obtain may be the main reason for selecting this cut. By the way, this may be somewhat confusing but the word *prime* in *prime rib* does not mean USDA prime grade (the highest grade); it means only that it's the most desirable part of the rib section. It is prime *grade* only if the USDA designation PRIME is stamped on. In fact, most prime rib roasts sold in grocery stores are *choice grade*, not *prime grade*.

- If a dry-aged beef roast is the goal, rib roast is one of the best, but any cut of beef commonly used for beef roast will do: chuck, rump, round, eye of round, or tri-tip roast, for example. Many people naturally prefer to cook these cuts of dry-aged beef as roasts, but they can also be cut and cooked as steak.

THE AGING TIME FOR BEEF

At the beginning of this chapter, it was pointed out that beef could be aged longer than other kinds of meat because it's highest in saturated fats and thus more resistant to developing a rancid taste due to oxidation of the fat. This information was not necessarily meant to suggest that the meat be dry aged for a long time when you process it for the first time. If the dry-aging period is too long, the meat might have too strong a taste for you and your family or friends to eat. Below I will give you some guidelines to help decide the aging period for the first batch. These guidelines are based on comments by numerous dry-age practitioners.

Most people who eat beef that has been aged two weeks find it to be more tender and tastier than steak that has not been dry aged, and most people will not detect any unusual or objectionable taste. Almost everyone who has eaten dry-aged steak would rather have steak aged two weeks than unaged steak. Between about six weeks and eight weeks, a richer taste develops that people have variously described as *nutty, cheesy,* or *beefy.* Also, the steak becomes juicier because the weakened connective tissue causes the meat to shrink less during cooking. Well over 50 percent of the tasters found these flavors and increased juiciness to be pleasant or delightful.

The flavors that develop after about nine weeks are found to be unpleasant by most people, but there are individuals who consider aging less than nine weeks to be too short. The word *funky* is often used to describe these flavors. People who like them often say "funky" with a smile, and those who do not say "funky" with a frown.

The rind and fat cap are always trimmed off before the beef is cooked and served, but removal of the bone is optional. Since most of the funkiness is concentrated on or near the surface of the meat, the removal of the fat cap and rind gets rid of much the aroma. However, if the bone is left attached, it will carry a considerable amount of funky odor to the dinner table.

COOKING BEEF STEAK OR ROAST

After investing the time and money required to dry age the beef, it would be a shame if it were not cooked properly. Invest a little more time to read good recipes on how to cook beefsteaks and roasts. And if you do not have one, invest a few dollars in a meat thermometer. Beef lovers, especially lovers of dry-aged beef, usually say that the beef is best when it is cooked no more than medium rare, which is 130 to 140°F (54.4–60.0°C). If the meat rests for 10 minutes or so after it reaches a certain temperature, the internal temperature will rise a few degrees. If this fact is kept in mind, there is less chance that the meat will be overcooked.

CHAPTER 7

Dry-Aged Big Game

COMPARING BEEF WITH VENISON

Important Point: This chapter provides information about dry-aged big game. Chapter 12 will show you, step by step, how to dry age big game, venison, or *any other kind of meat.*

Originally, the word *venison* meant the meat of any large game animal. Nowadays, in American English, the word usually refers to the meat of a deer, but a few of us use the word, occasionally, to mean the meat of any big-game animal that is roughly similar to a deer (elk, moose, caribou, antelope, reindeer, et cetera). For this chapter, please allow me to use the word *venison* in this way.

It is safe to say that venison is more like beef than the meat of any other species of domesticated animal. And since beef is dry aged more than any other meat, the dry aging of venison will be compared with, and based on, the dry aging of beef. We will see, however, that the dry aging of beef is much less complicated than the dry aging of venison.

The meat from commercially raised beef cattle that will be eaten as steaks or roasts is rather uniform compared with the meat from venison. The domesticated animals are normally the same age range and are the same species even though there are numerous breeds.

(Of course, elderly dairy cows that are ground into hamburger when they are too old to produce milk are not included in this comparison.) The big-game animals, though, are of various species and have a much wider age range.

We know that the diet of cattle can vary, but we also know that the diet of venison—even two animals of the same species—can differ even more than that of cattle. It is well known that the texture and flavor of the meat is affected by the diet.

Beef cattle are slaughtered quickly and efficiently to prevent the adrenaline rush and stress that adversely affects the meat. On the other hand, big-game animals are often excited before death.

Beef cattle are quickly eviscerated, but it may be impossible to remove the innards of venison quickly. The carcass of a steer or heifer is skinned and chilled soon—sometimes within minutes of being dispatched—but that of a large game animal may hang, unavoidably, from the branch of a tree until transportation can be arranged. Prompt evisceration and skinning begins the cooling process for both domesticated beef cattle and game, and cooling all carcasses quickly is a good practice whether dry aging is planned or not.

The sanitation practices at modern, commercial cattle slaughterhouses in the United States far surpass the those employed by the average venison hunter. For big game dressed in the field, the sanitation is normally substandard, and the butchering is often done at an ambient temperature that exceeds what's allowed in a commercial slaughterhouse.

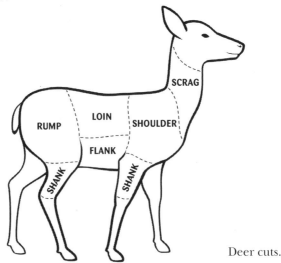

Deer cuts.

AGING CONSIDERATIONS FOR VENISON

We normally think that *aging* occurs with the passage of *time*, but the aging of meat is not only the result of the elapse of time. Aging also has been correctly called *ripening, conditioning,* or even *seasoning.* These words correctly apply because the process that we are talking about is a complex series of physical and chemical changes in the muscle tissue caused by a combination of time and storage temperature. This series of changes result in ripening, conditioning, and seasoning of the meat, causing taste changes. Temperatures higher than 34 to 38°F (1–3°C) will cause the *aging/ripening/conditioning/seasoning* to proceed much faster than advisable. For many things, we human beings often believe that faster is usually better. Faster is not necessarily better for dry aging.

When we dry age beef, we are normally using the meat from young animals that are (compared with wild big game) very similar to one another. Also, roughly the same slaughtering practices, butchering practices, sanitation practices, and meat preservation practices have been applied to each of these domesticated bovines. As indicated in the previous section, *Comparing Beef with Venison,* when we dry age big game this is clearly not the case; there are many reasons why the meat from one animal can be dissimilar to that of another. Consequently, all possible variables for the quality of venison from *each* animal must be judged to determine if it is a candidate for dry aging.

CAN THIS VENISON BE DRY AGED?

When determining if a cut of venison can be dry aged, initially the same considerations that were applicable for beef should be applied to the hunk of venison. (It may be helpful to review chapter 6, especially the section titled *Selecting a Cut of Beef.*) These considerations are as follows:

- If steaks are desired, can this cut of meat be cooked satisfactorily with quick-cooking methods? (If the animal is young, and if the cut is from the same part of the animal that is used for *beefsteaks,* the cut of venison passes this suitability test.)

- If a dry-aged roast is desired, the cut of meat can be dry aged if it has the appropriate size and shape. For example, a cut of venison can be dry aged for a roast if it is large and thick. If it is small and thin, the roast will disappear when the rind is trimmed off. (Many venison cooks believe that venison need not be dry aged if it is to be roasted; tenderness can be accomplished by moist and slow roasting, and the gamy taste provides the special flavor.)
- As indicated in the previous chapter, *Dry-Aged Beef*, it is advantageous if some of the outside surface has a layer of fat on top, and/or some of the surface is protected by bone (chine bone, for example). Wild game normally has less fat than domesticated animals, and there will probably be no bone unless the animal was professionally butchered with special instructions. Having this surface protection helps to make the cut suitable for dry aging. (This protection of the outside surface results in less drying of the surface and less trimming of red-meat rind.)
- The venison should be fresh and clean. It might not be as fresh as a subprimal cut of domesticated meat that you just got at the butcher shop, but if it is relatively clean and fresh it can be dry aged.
- The candidacy for dry aging is also dependent on the size and thickness of the cut of venison. It was pointed out directly above that surface fat and surface bone will result in less wasteful trimming of the rind. Well, the greater the volume and thickness, the less wasteful the trimming of the rind; if the cut of meat is large and thick, the discarded rind will be a small percent of the total.

If you decide to dry age your venison, review the dry-aging information in chapter 5, and use chapter 12 to provide step-by-step dry-aging directions.

DESELECTING VENISON FOR DRY AGING

In some conditions and situations, dry aging venison might be ill advised. This requires case-by-case personal judgment and there are no strict rules, but the following guidelines should help to decide *against* dry aging when that decision is best.

- Meat from extremely young big game (less than one year old) is invariably tender and juicy, and there would likely not be significant improvement from dry aging. Dry aging might improve the flavor, but the result might not be worth the effort and might not be appreciated.

- Any experienced hunter knows that after the animal is down, the real work begins. Cooling the meat is the most important thing to do. Gutting—and in some cases bleeding—is first. This is usually done in the field, and the hide is commonly left on until you reach camp. Leaving the hide on helps to protect the meat from bugs and dirt. After the hide is removed, the carcass is put in a game bag to protect the meat from insects and contamination. Ideally the carcass should be hung quickly in a cool place or in a rented nearby meat locker. If one or more of the good handling practices mentioned here were omitted, a decision to skip dry aging would be in order.

- Even if the animal was harvested during cool or chilly weather, if it was kept at the campsite for a week it should not be dry aged because significant or adequate dry aging has already taken place. Whenever the temperature is higher than the freezing point, dry aging begins. When the temperature is above 40°F (4.5°C), the dry-aging speed is excessive.

- An animal that was stressed before being harvested should not be dry aged. The reason for this is that the stress causes the sources of energy to be consumed instead of undergoing the normal conversion to lactic acid. The reduction of lactic acid allows bacteria to proliferate; this will likely result in spoilage of the meat if it is dry aged.

- Meat that will be ground, or processed into sausage, should not be dry aged. The grinding tenderizes the meat; additionally, ground meat and sausage taste better if made with fresh meat.

- Most people believe that the main reason for dry aging venison is to make it more tender. As mentioned above, many people consider it inadvisable and unnecessary to dry age any cut of venison that will undergo a moist and lengthy cooking method. Such cooking, they believe, will accomplish the desired tenderization.

DRY-AGING TIME FOR VENISON

The muscle tissue of big-game animals is tough because the animals are constantly using their muscles. Compared to domesticated animals, it is said that wild animals are like Olympic athletes. If that is true, we might say that domesticated animals are like couch potatoes, and the muscles are, therefore, more tender.

It is well known that the aging of meat tenderizes it, and for most hunters tenderization is the main reason wild game is aged. The second reason is to make it moister. The changing of flavor never seems to be mentioned as a reason for dry aging venison. Most hunters appear to be satisfied with the funky, gamy taste—or, possibly, they simply endure it. Maybe they do not want to add another exotic taste to that which is already there.

With beef, the fact that rather lengthy dry aging will impart an appealing nutty, cheesy, or ultra-beefy flavor seems to be the top reason for aging it. Very long dry aging that gives the beef a "funky" taste appeals to many people—but certainly not to most people. Dry aging beef to make it more tender and moist are the second and third reasons.

Nowadays, hunting ranches that cater to hunters for a fee are quite common. They are most common in states where there is relatively little public land—Texas, for example. These places always have coolers for storing the game animals that have been harvested. Some hunting ranches will transport the animals to special facilities to eviscerate them, skin them, help bone them, and put them in the cooler. If the harvested game is cared for under these conditions, more of the game meat can be selected for dry aging.

As I've mentioned, even if a big-game animal is suitable for dry aging, there are no hard-and-fast rules for the best length of time, but there some aging suggestions below. Personal preferences for aging time have been put aside. In general, quarter cuts are dry aged longer than the smaller muscle groups. Some non-venison meats are included.

SUGGESTED DRY-AGE TIMES FOR VARIOUS GAME

- Elk, moose: 10–14 days
- Deer, caribou, sheep, antelope, goat: 7–10 days
- Wild boar, feral pigs: 4–8 days

CHAPTER 8

Dry-Aged Duck

Important Point: This chapter provides information about dry-aged duck. Chapter 12 will show you, step by step, how to dry age duck or *any other kind of meat.*

The dry aging of any kind meat is not difficult, but it is time consuming. Therefore, we have the right to expect a reward for the effort expended. The reward for dry aging duck is that we can eat and serve an exotic, tender, and gourmet meat that has a mild and pleasant flavor and the easy-on-the-eye color of veal. The alternative is to avoid the effort of dry aging and endure the normally earthy, gamy, muddy flavor of the tough meat, or mask it with strong marinades and sauces.

For me, one of the greatest mysteries in the craft of dry aging is that many people, including myself, find dry-aged duck delightful, but dry-aged chicken does not engender a smidgeon of excitement. There are numerous differences in the composition of the dark muscle meat of the duck compared with the light colored muscle meat of the chicken. Is the difference in the appeal of the dry-aged birds related to this? Is it related to the higher amount of polyunsaturated fats in chicken? It seems that food science has not yet explained this disparity.

This chapter focuses on the dry aging of domesticated ducks, and this dry aging normally takes place with the skin, legs, and wings intact. As suggested below, the dry aging of a whole, fully plucked and eviscerated domesticated duck will produce the best results. Even though a whole bird is best for dry aging, it is much better for dry aging if it's butterflied and flattened. This is accomplished by either removing the spine or cutting through the bird along one side of the breast keel bone.

If a fowl is flattened, all surfaces will receive about the same airflow while being dry aged. And if the airflow is uniform, the thorough drying of the surfaces thwarts spoilage.

In this chapter, the duck will be butterflied and flattened by removing the spine. In the following chapter, the goose will be butterflied by cutting through the fowl along one side of the breast keel bone. The method the practitioner chooses is largely personal preference.

It should be noted, however, that a bird flattened by the spine-removal method could occupy a little less area than one flattened by cutting along the keel bone. The main reason for this is that when the spine is removed and the bird is flattened, the legs *can* be positioned inward with the drumsticks close to and parallel with each other. However, when the bird is butterflied by cutting along its keel bone, the legs always flail outward to the left and right. This flailing requires more room to the left and right. This might be important if limited refrigerator shelf space is a consideration.

When the modern dry-aging technique that is used for domesticated ducks is also used for wild ducks, certain conditions will have to be met in order to get acceptable results. For example, preparing the wild duck to be dry aged must result in the bird being plucked and must result in the skin covering being intact. Many hunters do not like to pluck wild ducks because it is difficult and time consuming, so they skin the whole bird. This is not acceptable preparation for the dry-aging method described in this book because the red meat needs the protection afforded by the skin.

Some hunters might pluck only the breast—which is not too difficult. This is acceptable if nothing but the breast is dry aged and if the skin on the breast is intact. *If the dry-aging procedure described below is used, the red meat of the duck must be completely covered by plucked skin; this skin is required to prevent the edible muscle tissue from drying.*

When either domesticated or wild ducks are dry aged, as described below, the exposed surface of the fowl dries into a covering called the *rind* or *crust*. If this exposed surface is skin—and most of it is—this skin will become rind, and it is removed and discarded before eating the muscle meat.

The result is that most of the top surface of the red meat will be protected by the dried skin (and the underlying layer of fat) while it is being dry aged and cooked. (Please keep in mind that *all* muscle tissue in a duck is *red* meat; ducks do not have white breast meat.)

Because it is essential to have the skin intact when dry aging ducks, many hunters, as mentioned above, will age only the easily plucked breasts. If only the breasts are dry aged, what is to be done with the remaining parts of the skinned duck? Well, these parts can be used in recipes that employ moist cooking methods (stew-like dishes and soups, for example). If you would like to make soup with the leftover wings, legs, et cetera, please consider the recipe near the end of this chapter; it is appropriately called *Duck Soup.* As the name implies, it is very easy to make.

Alternatively, you can master moderately efficient techniques for plucking a whole wildfowl by watching presentations on YouTube, for example, and then, for that wild duck, you can dry age and cook it as you would domesticated duck. The difficulty of removing all of the feathers from the wildfowl is the only thing that hinders the application of modern dry-aging techniques.

Pekin ducks. The most common domesticated meat duck.
One male (back) and two females (foreground). *Photo courtesy www.countryfarm-lifestyles.com.*

The domesticated duck that I recommend for dry aging is the breed most commonly available in the supermarkets in the United States and Canada, the Pekin duck. (*Pekin* duck is a *breed* of duck, but *Peking* duck is a method of cooking duck that originated in Beijing, China. *Peking* is a historical way to write *Beijing*.) Pekin strain ducks are noted for being large and for having a thick layer of fat under the skin. When processed for market, the ducklings are about seven or eight weeks old, and the dressed weight is about 4½ to 5½ pounds (2.0–2.5 kg).

Ducks have a high bone-to-meat ratio, so a 5-pound (2.3 kg) duck will not feed as many people as a 5-pound chicken. As the main course, a duck this size will normally serve two or three people. As a side dish, it may serve four to five people.

HOW TO BUTTERFLY A RAW DUCK

I believe that the following method of preparing a bird for dry aging is best for the following reasons (these reasons were discussed above, but they are being mentioned again to explain some important details):

- Butterflying and flattening the bird is infinitely better than leaving it whole ("in the round"). This is because the air circulation over both the outer surface (skin) and the inner surface (cavity) of the flattened bird will be effective and uniform. And if the air circulation is good and uniform, the chances of spoilage or fungal development are greatly reduced because a protective rind will form over the entire surface.
- Leaving the wings and legs attached increases the amount of dry-aged meat available for cooking and eating.
- Because the legs and wings are not removed, less of the delicious and edible red meat is exposed to the air and wastefully dried up into inedible rind.

Step-by-Step Cutting Instructions for a Duck

Note: *The following cutting instructions describe how to butterfly a domesticated or wild duck by cutting out the spine and flattening the carcass. The same technique can be used for a goose. Alternatively, either fowl can be cut along the left or right side of the keel bone—then the carcass can be opened and flattened (see the instructions for butterflying a goose in the next chapter).*

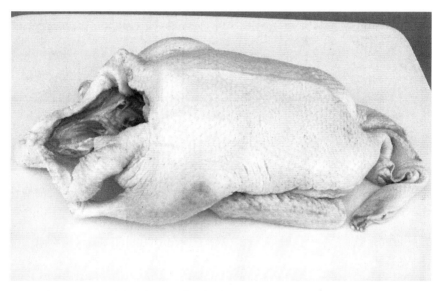

Rinse the cavity and the skin of the duck. Pat the cavity and the skin dry with paper towels or a clean cloth.

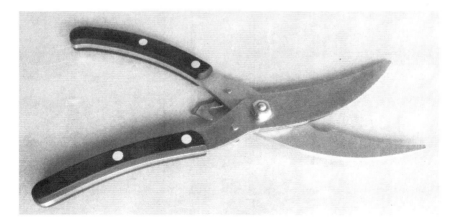

Poultry shears–also called poultry scissors. (There is notch toward the back of the lower blade. This notch is helpful to grasp, hold, and cut small bones.)

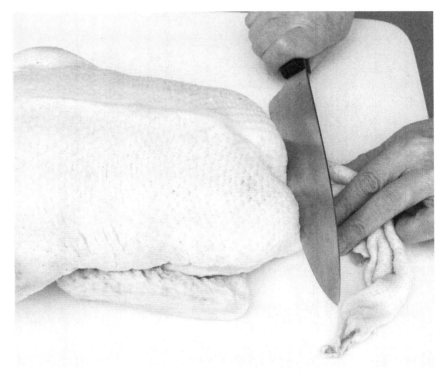

Trim the excess neck skin, but leave enough skin to cover the red muscle tissue. Discard this skin, or throw it in your stockpot.

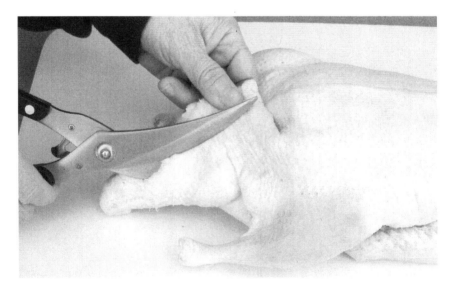

Trim off and discard the excess cavity skin. Be sure to leave enough skin to cover the red meat.

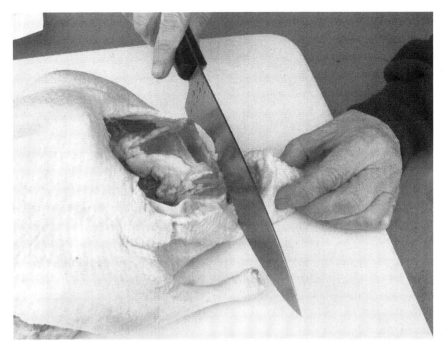

Cut off about 2 inches (5 cm) of the tail and discard it or throw it in the stockpot.

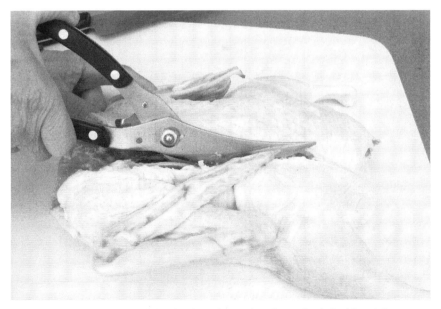

Cut from the neck area of the bird to the cavity along the left side of the spine.

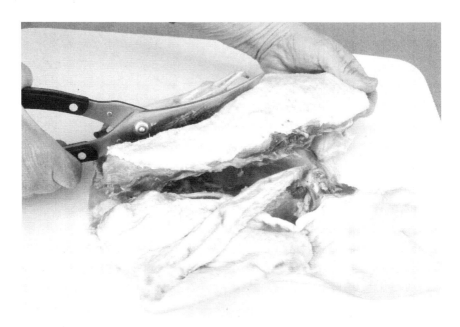

Cut from the neck area of the bird to the cavity along the right side of the spine. The spine will now be free from the bird.

Remove the backbone and butterfly the duck. (Force the carcass open with your thumbs.) Removal of the spine and butterflying is called *spatchcocking*.

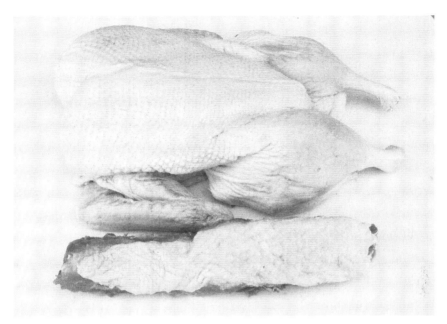

The spatchcock has been completed. Breast of duck is shown. Instead of throwing the backbone away, you might want to throw it in your stockpot and make Duck Soup.

THE DUCK DRY-AGING PROCESS

The dry-aging process for ducks is essentially the same as for meats such as lamb or beef. Please follow the instructions in chapter 12, and monitor the temperature and humidity. Reviewing appropriate parts of chapter 5 would also be helpful.

Important point: Because ducks and geese are usually butterflied before dry aging, the skins of the upper thighs may lay flat against the belly skin when the butterflied bird is placed either upright or upside down on the drying rack. This contact of the thigh skin with the belly skin might prevent the required drying and cause putrefaction. I suggest that some suitable method be used to separate the thighs from the belly skin to facilitate drying and rind formation. One way to accomplish this is to use several round toothpicks as "pillars" between the thigh and the belly.

The ideal aging time, as mentioned before, is a matter of personal preference. However, for a domesticated duck of the size commonly sold in a grocery store (4½ to 5½ pounds, or 2.0–2.5 kg), I recommend that you age your first duck for 7 to 10 days. If the result is less than perfect, please change the dry-aging time to suit your taste.

The paragraph above suggests the approximate length of the dry-aging time. Another way to determine when to stop the dry aging is to squeeze the breast between your thumb and index finger. If the breast gives way to the pressure, it indicates that the tough fibers have broken down and collagen has gelatinized. When this "pinch test" is positive, the dry aging can be discontinued. If the breast recovers immediately from the pinch, the bird needs to be aged a little longer.

Wild birds are usually smaller than the domesticated ones sold in grocery stores. Because of that, and because they usually have already received some in-the-field-and-out-of-the-refrigerator aging, the dry-aging time is less. (In chapter 5, please review the last two paragraphs in the section *Aging Time.*) As with domesticated birds, the dry aging may begin either when the bird is fresh or after it has been thawed. I suggest that a wild mallard should be aged four to seven days. (If considerable time has passed between the shooting of the bird and its refrigeration, the aging time should be shortened, or it might even be best if the bird is deselected for dry aging.) As mentioned above, wild birds, too, should be dry aged with the skin on. If the bird is without skin, the flesh will dry too fast, requiring the red meat to be trimmed off and wasted. Of course, the pinch test can also be used on wild waterfowl.

COOKING THE DUCK

This book is intended to be a manual for dry aging various kinds of meats; it is not intended to be a cookbook for dry-aged meats. However, the two chapters on dry-aged waterfowl seem to beg some attention to the cooking of these birds. The reason is this: With the exception of ducks and geese, all of the dry-aged meats discussed in this book are trimmed and the rind (crust) is shaved off before cooking. After removal of the rind, the meat can be cooked in almost any way imaginable; special treatment is not required. The waterfowl, on the other hand, are usually *cooked with the rind in place*, and then the rind (skin and fat—and some bone) is removed and discarded before the muscle meat is eaten.

Normally, the skin of waterfowl is considered a very edible part of the bird. Indeed, in the case of the famous dish known as *Peking Duck*, the truly authentic Chinese presentations of this dish are mostly thin, crisp skin with very little meat. In fact, prior to cooking the *Peking Duck*, air is blown under the skin with a bamboo tube; this causes the skin to balloon and separate from the duck's body, and this ballooned skin becomes crispy while roasting. It is the crispy skin that is cherished by the fans of *Peking Duck*. (Nowadays, a mechanical or electric air pump usually replaces the bamboo tube.) Unfortunately, the roasted skin of a dry-aged duck is likely to be too hard and strong-tasting to eat. As mentioned previously, the rind of dry-aged meat tends to acquire a strong aroma and taste (in this case, the skin of the duck is the rind).

The recipe below is my creation, and it is for seasoning roasted dry-aged duck. It was originally a recipe for hot smoking domesticated ducks. The recipe was changed slightly to make it suitable for any dry-aged waterfowl that will be roasted in a common oven.

If you try this recipe—or even just look it over—I believe that you will conclude that many recipes can be adapted to dry-aged waterfowl. The cooking website *allrecipes.com, for example*, lists about 70 recipes for cooking duck; many can be used for dry-aged duck.

Delightful Duck

It is assumed that the dry aging has been finished and that the bird is ready to season and cook. This section of the chapter will guide you as you season and cook the duck while using the dry-rub recipe below.

It is important that the amount of dry-rub seasoning mixture is appropriate for the weight of the duck, so the duck must be weighed *after* the dry aging is finished. (If the amount of seasoning is off, the duck will be either too highly seasoned or inadequately seasoned.)

Below, you will notice that the dry-rub seasoning sufficient to season 2 pounds (900 g) of duck contains salt, sugar, and eight varieties of herbs and spices (10 items, altogether). And you will notice that the total quantity (volume) of this dry-rub mixture for seasoning 2 pounds of duck is indicated at the bottom of this seasoning list: 10 teaspoons. *In other words, 5 teaspoons of the dry-rub seasoning mixture is required for every pound of duck.*

Your duck will most likely weigh 4½ to 5½ pounds (2.0–2.5 kg). If it weighs 5¼ pounds, for instance, you will need *5.25 × 5 teaspoons = 26.25 teaspoons* of seasoning. Now, since there are 24 teaspoons in a ½-cup measuring cup, 26.25 teaspoons is equal to ½ cup + 2¼ teaspoons. So, ½ cup + 2¼ teaspoons of dry-rub seasoning is exactly the right amount for a 5¼-pound duck. The easiest way to season your 5¼-pound duck is to make three batches of the dry-rub mixture (enough for 6 pounds of duck), use ½ cup + 2¼ teaspoons for your duck, and then save the leftover dry rub for the next time you process a duck. *(Normally, in this book, metric equivalents for all US measuring units are provided for the convenience of individuals who have not mastered our awkward measuring system. In this paragraph, however, providing the metric equivalents was not done in all cases because it would give a cluttered appearance. If conversion is necessary, conversion tables are available in appendix 2.)*

Is it truly necessary to do all this measuring and calculating? It all depends on your mindset. If you want your results to be predictable, if you want to duplicate the same great product you made last time, if you want to avoid throwing a $100 hunk of meat in the garbage, then—yes—in my opinion, all of this measuring is necessary. Television celebrity chefs seem to prepare fantastically delicious food by using a "handful of this," a "small pinch of that," and a "splash of whatever." Unfortunately, I am not a culinary artist, so I do not have the skills to season in this manner. The combination of my lack of culinary artistic skills and my personal mindset does not permit me to forgo measuring. Nevertheless, the culinary-artist approach might be best for you.

THE DRY-RUB SEASONING FOR 2 POUNDS (900 G) OF DUCK

3 teaspoons (15 ml) salt
2 teaspoons (10 ml) granulated sugar
1 teaspoon (5 ml) poultry seasoning—packed in the spoon
1 teaspoon (5 ml) onion powder (or granules)
½ teaspoon (2.5 ml) paprika
½ teaspoon (2.5 ml) dried sage, rubbed—packed in the spoon
½ teaspoon (2.5 ml) dried marjoram or dried oregano

½ teaspoon (2.5 ml) ground thyme
½ teaspoon (2.5 ml) white pepper
½ teaspoon (2.5 ml) garlic powder (or granules)
TOTAL: 10 teaspoons (50 ml)

Calculate and measure the dry-rub seasoning ingredients into a small bowl. Mix until uniform and set aside.

Day 1
1. Place the duck in a food container made of food-grade plastic or stainless steel. The container must have an airtight lid, or plastic food wrap must be used to provide an airtight cover.
2. Use something like a basting brush or a clean cloth to apply a coating of water to all surfaces of the bird. (This coating will jump-start the dissolving of seasonings, and the dissolved salt will help to extract more moisture from the meat. That moisture will dissolve even more seasonings and make this seasoning available to flavor the duck.)
3. Mix the seasoning thoroughly, and apply it to all surfaces of the bird. Place the lid or plastic wrap on the food container to prevent evaporation of the moisture. Refrigerate the duck for six days. Don clean rubber gloves several times during this period and rub all surfaces of the fowl to redistribute the dry-rub mixture.

Day 6
1. Rinse the duck *very well* with cool water. (All seasoning should be rinsed from the surface of the bird.) Blot it with paper towels.
2. Wrap the whole bird with paper towels, and wrap it again with newspaper. (The paper wrap is applied to absorb excessive water.)
3. Preferably, the seasoned fowl should be stored in the refrigerator overnight. During this overnight period, the seasoning tends to migrate and become uniform, and the excess water is absorbed by the paper that was used for wrapping.

Day 7
1. Preheat the kitchen oven to 350°F (175°C). Place the duck on an elevated wire rack in a roasting pan. The pan should be at least

1 inch (2.5 cm) deep—a little deeper is better. *Placement on an elevated wire rack within a pan is important.* The high oven temperature will cause a large amount of fat to melt, and this grease will collect in the bottom of the pan; if the duck is not on an elevated rack, parts of the duck will be submerged in melted fat.

2. Most people say that duck tastes best when the meat is still pink after cooking. And most connoisseurs like it to be cooked medium rare: 130–140°F (54.4–60.0°C). The USDA (United States Department of Agriculture) says that poultry (either wild or domesticated) will be safe to eat if it has reached an internal temperature of 165°F (74°C) throughout. However, culinary experts who specialize in duck cookery disagree with the USDA and claim that they are unable to find any records of illness caused by eating medium-rare duck, but they acknowledge the documented danger of eating medium-rare chicken. I have always eaten duck medium rare, and I will continue to do so. Nevertheless, I completely sympathize with individuals who follow the USDA guidelines. Anyway, no matter what you decide is best for you, you will need an instant-read thermometer or a cable probe thermometer. Insert the thermometer probe in the thickest part of the breast. The cable probe thermometer is easy to use and is very convenient because the oven need not be opened to check the temperature. It is highly recommended.

3. If the surface color of the bird begins to darken and become unattractive while it is roasting, cover it with a loose aluminum-foil tent.

4. Roast the duck until the internal temperature reaches a few degrees below your preference, and then remove it from the oven. The temperature will continue to climb 5 to 10°F (3–5°C) after the duck is removed.

5. After the roasted bird has cooled a few minutes, use culinary scissors to cut away and discard the skin. If any muscle fiber was exposed, it will have become obviously inedible rind. Shave off and discard this muscle fiber, too.

6. Carve and serve the muscle meat of the duck as you would serve any roasted fowl.

DUCK SOUP

This soup is based on a Chinese recipe that I found in a cookbook published in Hong Kong. It takes only a few minutes of work to make a very delicious and unique soup.

Duck bones (use the bones remaining after the duck is carved, but avoid using rind that is stuck to the bones, and do not use bones that have been directly exposed to the dry-aging air)

1 each: duck heart, gizzard, and neck, but *not* the liver (scraps from the wings and legs—raw or cooked—can be used; do not fret if some of the giblets are not available)

1½ quarts (1½ liters) water

4 green onions, roughly chopped

1 tablespoon (15 ml) sherry (dry or medium) or *shao hsing* wine (optional)

1 or 2 teaspoons (5–10 ml) grated fresh ginger *or* ¼ teaspoon (1.25 ml) ginger powder (fresh ginger, grated, is preferred)

6 teaspoons of Chinese-style chicken stock powder *or* 5 bouillon cubes, chicken flavor

1 heaping tablespoon cornstarch mixed into a slurry with 3 tablespoons water. (This cornstarch slurry is optional, but recommended, for thickening the soup.)

1. Put all ingredients *except for the cornstarch slurry* in a pot, and simmer at least 1 hour. (If possible, it is best to make this soup stock a day before it is to be served; it should be chilled overnight to facilitate the removal of fat and scum.)
2. Strain the soup into another pan. If froth or scum forms on the surface, skim it off. Discard the bones and the green onions. Save the heart, gizzard, and neck to use as a snack—or mince this meat and add it to the strained broth. Save the leg and wing scraps for a snack, or mince the scraps and return to the pot.
3. Add 1 cup (240 ml) of very thinly sliced celery to the broth, and simmer a few minutes until the celery is barely tender.
4. If desired, thicken the soup by slowly adding the cornstarch slurry while stirring until the desired thickness is achieved. Serve.

CHAPTER 9

Dry-Aged Goose

Important Point: This chapter provides information about dry-aged goose. Chapter 12 will show you, step-by-step, how to dry-age goose or *any other kind of meat.*

The dry aging of ducks and geese is very similar, but there are enough differences to warrant a separate chapter for each. This chapter is devoted to the goose.

In this chapter, the words *goose* and *geese* are used often. But in most cases, the rarely heard words *gosling* and *goslings* are more precise. Goslings are young geese. And when we shop for *geese,* goslings are usually the birds sold (or special-ordered) in a grocery store or in an ethnic meat market in the United States. The dressed weight of a gosling is about 8 to 12 pounds (3.6–5.5 kg).

This chapter focuses on the dry aging of domesticated geese (goslings), and this dry aging normally takes place with the skin, legs, and wings intact. As suggested below, the dry aging of a whole, fully plucked and eviscerated *domesticated* gosling will definitely produce the best results.

It is imperative that the goose be butterflied and flattened before dry aging. This is accomplished by either removing the spine or cutting through the bird along one side of the breast keel bone. The arguments for butterflying and flattening the bird as opposed to leaving the bird "in the round" can be found in chapter 8, *Dry-Aged Duck*, in the section titled *How to Butterfly a Raw Duck.*

If a fowl is flattened, all surfaces will receive about the same airflow while being dry aged. And if the airflow is uniform, the thorough drying of the surfaces helps to prevent spoilage and helps to stop fungal development on the surface.

In this chapter, the goose will be butterflied and flattened by cutting along one side of the breast keel bone. In the preceding chapter, the duck was butterflied and flattened by removing the spine. The method you choose is largely personal preference.

A bird flattened by the spine-removal method occupies a little less area than one flattened by cutting along one side of the breast keel bone. If you wish to explore this method of flattening, please read the explanation in the introduction to chapter 8.

When the modern dry-aging technique that is used for domesticated geese is also used for wild geese, certain conditions will have to be met in order to get acceptable results. For example, the preparation of the wild goose to be dry aged must result in the bird being plucked and must result in the skin covering being intact. Many hunters do not like to pluck wild geese because it is difficult and time consuming, so they skin the whole bird. This is not acceptable preparation for the dry-aging method described in this book: The red meat needs the protection afforded by the skin.

You may recall that similar statements were made in chapter 8. Because of the great similarity between ducks and geese, either this information must be repeated or you must be referred to chapter 8 countless times. I have decided that repeating the information, but condensing when possible, will be easier and more comfortable. I hope you agree.

Some hunters might pluck only the breast—which is not too difficult. This is acceptable if only the breast is to be dry aged. The breast of a goose can be separated from the rest of the carcass and dry aged if its skin is intact, and if the red meat is covered by the skin.

The rind or crust (consisting mainly of dried skin that develops when geese are dry aged) should be left in place while cooking, but removed before eating. The result is that most of the red meat will be protected by the dried skin (and the underlying fat) while it is being dry aged and cooked. (Please keep in mind that *all* muscle tissue in a goose is *red* meat; neither geese nor ducks have white breast meat.)

Because it is necessary to have the skin intact when dry aging geese, many hunters, as mentioned above, will age only the easily plucked breasts of wild geese. If only the breasts are dry aged, the remaining parts can be used in recipes that employ various cooking methods—soups, stewed dishes, or even ground goose recipes, for example. If you would like to make soup with the leftover wings, legs, et cetera, please consider the *Duck Soup* recipe near the end of chapter 8; it is very easy to make; simply substitute goose meat for the duck meat and change the name to *Goose Soup*.

Moderately efficient techniques for plucking a wild goose can be mastered by watching presentations on YouTube, for example, and then the same procedure for dry aging and cooking whole domesticated geese can be used.

The domesticated geese that are offered at reputable stores (or ordered from reputable dealers) will be one of several species that have a good reputation for culinary applications. The breed most commonly sold in the in the United States is the Embden goose. The small to medium-sized Embden gosling commonly retailed in the US will weigh 8 to 12 pounds (3.6–5.5 kg).

The Embden goose. (Also spelled Emden.) Embden geese are one of the most common breeds raised for meat production. *Photo courtesy Hays Cummins.*

Geese, like ducks, have a high bone-to-meat ratio, so a 10-pound (4.6 kg) goose will not feed as many people as a 10-pound turkey. As the main course, a goose this size will serve six to eight.

If you have never eaten goose, you might be interested to know that most people, including myself, say that the taste of goose is much more like beef than like any kind of fowl.

HOW TO BUTTERFLY A RAW GOOSE

The instructions below show how to prepare a raw, domesticated goose for dry aging. The cutting instructions also apply to a wild goose that has been completely plucked and has all the skin remaining.

I believe this method of preparing a bird for dry aging is best for the following reasons:

- Butterflying the bird is better than leaving it whole and in the round because the air circulation over the outer surface and inner surface (cavity) of the flattened bird will be uniform.
- If the air circulation is good, and if it is uniform, the chance of spoilage or fungal development is reduced because a protective rind will form over the entire surface.
- Leaving the wings and legs attached increases the amount of dry-aged meat available for cooking and eating.
- Because the legs and wings are not removed, less of the delicious and edible red meat is exposed to the air and wastefully dried up into inedible rind.

Step-by-Step Cutting Instructions for a Goose

Note: *The following cutting instructions describe how to butterfly a goose by cutting through the cavity along the left or right side of the keel bone, and then opening and flattening the carcass. The same technique can be used for a duck. Alternatively, either fowl can be butterflied and flattened by cutting out the spine and flattening the carcass. (Instructions for butterflying a duck by removing the spine, and a photo of the proper tool for butterflying a duck or a goose—"poultry shears"—appear in chapter 8, Step-by-Step Cutting Instructions for a Duck.)*

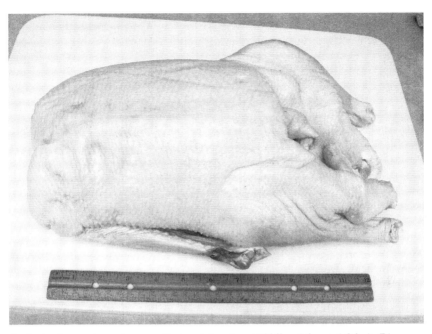

A whole domesticated goose that weighs about 9½ lbs. (about 4.3 kg). Rinse the cavity and the skin of the bird. Pat the cavity and the skin dry with paper towels or a clean cloth.

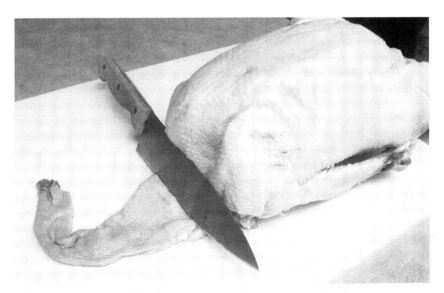

Trim the excess neck skin from the goose, but leave enough skin to cover the red muscle tissue. Discard this skin, or throw it in your stockpot.

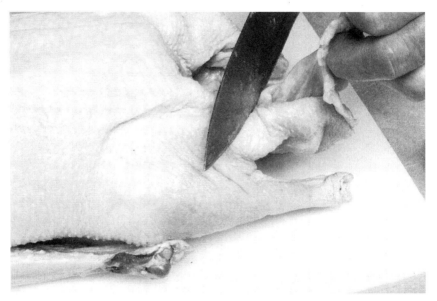

Trim off and discard the excess cavity skin from the goose. Be sure to leave enough skin to cover the red meat.

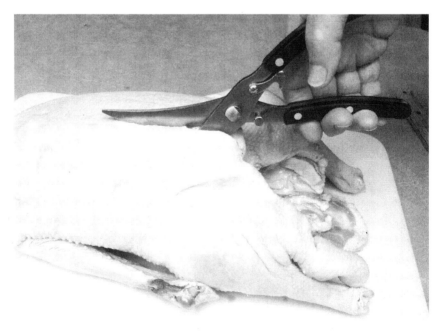

Cut from the cavity to the neck area of the bird along either the right or left side of the keel bone. Cut the flesh along the side of the keel bone deeply with a knife before using the poultry shears.

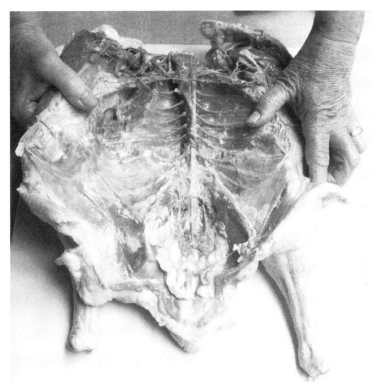

Spread the raw goose open to butterfly it and complete the spatch-cock. The carcass may be left as is, or the spine may be removed, too, as it was for the duck shown earlier in chapter 8.

Please keep in mind that if the butterflied goose is too large to fit on one shelf of the dry-aging refrigerator, it can be separated into two parts by removing the spine (*in addition to* making the described cut along the keel bone of the breast).

THE GOOSE DRY-AGING PROCESS

The dry-aging process for goose is essentially the same as for meats such as lamb or beef. Please follow the instructions in chapter 12 and monitor the temperature and humidity. Additional helpful information may be found in chapter 5.

Important point: Because ducks and geese are usually butterflied before dry aging, the skins of the upper thighs may lay flat against the belly skin when the butterflied bird is placed either upright or upside down on the drying rack. This contact of the thigh skin with the belly skin might prevent the required drying and cause putrefaction. I suggest that some suitable method be used to separate the thighs from the belly skin to facilitate drying and rind formation. One way to accomplish this is to use several round toothpicks as "pillars" between the thigh and the belly.

The ideal aging time, as mentioned before, is a matter of personal preference. However, I suggest that you try 14 to 21 days the first time. If the result is not exactly what you were expecting, please change the dry-aging time in the direction that will likely suit your taste.

The paragraph above suggests the approximate length of the dry-aging time. Another way to determine when to stop the dry aging is to squeeze the breast between your thumb and index finger. If the breast gives way to the pressure, it indicates that the tough fibers have broken down and collagen has gelatinized. When this "pinch test" is positive, the dry aging can be discontinued. If the breast recovers immediately from the pinch, the bird needs to be aged a little longer.

Wild birds are usually smaller than the domesticated ones sold in grocery stores. Because of that, and because they usually have already received some in-the-field-and-out-of-the-refrigerator aging, the dry-aging time is less. (In chapter 5, please review the last two paragraphs in the section *Aging Time.*)

As with domesticated birds, the dry aging of wild birds may begin either when the bird is fresh, or after it has been thawed. I suggest that a wild honker be aged 10 to 14 days. (If considerable time has passed between the shooting of the goose and its refrigeration, the aging time should be shortened.) As mentioned above, wild birds, too, should be dry aged with the skin on. If the bird is without skin, the flesh will dry and become hard, requiring it to be trimmed off and wasted. Of course, the pinch test can also be used on wild geese.

COOKING THE GOOSE

There is very little difference between cooking a domesticated goose and cooking a wild goose. Whether or not the domesticated or wild goose has been frozen and thawed also makes no difference. Finally, it makes very little difference whether or not the birds have been dry aged. The cooking website *allrecipes.com* lists about 30 recipes for cooking goose. Most of these recipes can be used for dry-aged goose.

Compared with a goose that was not dry aged, the skin of the roasted *dry-aged goose* will have a different texture. This is largely be due to the simple fact that it was dry aged, but to some extent it can be related to the *length of time* it was dry aged. Usually the skin of the dry-aged fowl will become hard, inedible rind. On the positive side, a dry-aged roasted goose will normally have better flavor and be more tender than goose that was not dry aged. The depth of flavor and tenderness are also related to the length of time the bird was dry aged; in general, the longer the aging, the more flavorful and tender the bird will be. Of course, if the dry-age time is excessive, the "deep flavor" may be a deep and unpleasant funky taste that some people do not enjoy.

GOLDEN GOOSE

This recipe, needless to say, requires a raw goose that has been previously butterflied and dry aged according to the applicable instructions in this chapter and in chapters 5 and 12.

This recipe will guide the marinating and cooking of the dry-aged goose. The marinade recipe is my own creation, but it is similar to some of the old-fashioned Yuletide goose seasonings.

Day 1, Morning, Preparing the Goose
1. Remove the bird's pinfeathers by using fish-boning tweezers, long-nose pliers, or common tweezers. (I prefer long-nose pliers.) Rinse well.
2. Refrigerate the butterflied goose while the marinade is being prepared.

Day 1, Morning (Continued), Marinade for Golden Goose
Prepare the following marinade for a 10-pound (4.5 kg) bird, but reduce the salt by 1 teaspoon (5 ml) for a 9-pound (4.1 kg) bird, and by 2 teaspoons (10 ml) for an 8-pound (3.6 kg) bird. However, if the bird has been pumped with a saltwater solution by the processor, start

out with 1 tablespoon (15 ml) of salt instead of 3 tablespoons (45 ml). (It is unlikely that the gosling was pumped with a saltwater solution. Turkeys, however, are sometimes pumped by the processor.)

3 tablespoons (45 ml) salt
¼ cup (60 ml) salad oil
2 cups (480 ml) chopped onions
1 cup (240 ml) prune juice
¾ cup (180 ml) sherry (dry or regular)
⅓ cup (80 ml) honey (if crystallized, liquefy by warming gently)
3 cloves garlic, minced
¼ cup (60 ml) soy sauce
2 teaspoons (10 ml) ground cayenne
1 teaspoon (5 ml) ground marjoram or ground oregano
1 teaspoon (5 ml) ground rosemary

Blend the marinade in a container large enough to hold the flattened goose. Stir until the salt and honey have dissolved.

The flattened goose may be cut in half down the spine if it will not fit in a container. See chapter 8 for spine-cutting instructions. Rub or brush the bird inside and out with the seasoning mixture (marinade). Cover and refrigerate.

A large and strong plastic bag may be used instead of a marinade container. If you do so, coat the bird with marinade by turning the bag over several times.

Day 2, Early Afternoon and Evening
Use something like a basting brush to reapply the marinade to all surfaces of the goose. Do this *at least* one time during the early-afternoon hours and *at least* one time during the evening hours. (If the goose is in a plastic bag, turn over the bag a few times.)

Day 3, Morning
Reapply the marinade as on day 2.

Day 3, Evening
Rinse the surfaces of the gosling briefly with cool water. Pat dry. Put the bird on a paper towel, skin-side up, and allow it to dry in the

refrigerator, uncovered, overnight. (In order to maintain the cleanliness of your dry aging refrigerator, your household refrigerator should be used for this.)

Day 4, Roasting the Goose

The estimated roasting time for a gosling weighing 8 to 10 pounds (3.6–4.5 kg) is 25 minutes per pound. Consequently, about 3 to 3½ hours will be required for an 8-pound gosling and a little over 4 hours will be necessary for a 10-pounder.

Geese are fatty birds, and much fat will melt and seep from the bird while it is roasting. If the proper precautions (listed below) are taken to prepare for dealing with melting fat, the roasting process will proceed smoothly.

- Use a large roasting pan that allows the flattened bird to lie skin-side up on a rack placed inside. (Because a butterflied goose requires a large area, it may be necessary to cut the bird in half and use two roasting pans.) The pan should be at least 1½ inches (3.5–4 cm) deep. If the rack is about 1 inch (2.5 cm) above the bottom of the pan, the goose will not touch the melted fat collecting there. It is not good for part of the goose to soak in melted fat while it is roasting. **Note:** *The rack will need to have legs that support it about 1 inch from the bottom of the pan, or some kind of makeshift supports will be needed.*
- It is convenient to insert a thermometer in the breast at this time. Make sure that the tip of the thermometer is buried in the center of a thick part of the breast. The tip should not be touching either bone or fat. The most convenient type of thermometer is a digital cooking thermometer with a cable: This shows the internal temperature of the bird without opening the oven door. There is a photo of this type of thermometer in chapter 2. An ovenproof meat thermometer will also work.
- Preheat the oven to 450°F (232°C).
- Reduce the heat to 350°F (176°C) and place the gosling in the oven.
- Check the appearance of the bird from time to time. If the skin begins to darken excessively while it is roasting, cover the bird loosely with an aluminum-foil tent. (The foil will deflect the heat and limit the darkening of the surface of the gosling.) It is also a

good idea to rotate (spin) the baking pan 180 degrees occasionally. (The reason for this is that an oven is often hotter in the back than it is near the pull-down door.)

- The bird is fully cooked when the internal temperature is 165°F (79°C). However, for many people, 180°F (82°C) is the traditional target for goose. Be aware that the internal temperature will climb 5 to 10°F (3–6°C) even after the bird is removed from the oven. Consequently, it is best to remove it from the oven when the internal temperature is a few degrees below the target temperature. When deciding the target temperature, please keep in mind that the 2014 guidelines published by the USDA state, *"Poultry products and wild birds are safe to eat if they are properly handled and cooked to a temperature of 165 degrees Fahrenheit (79 degrees Celsius)."* Despite these guidelines, some people prefer goose cooked medium rare, like duck—about 135°F (57°C).

- Let the goose set about 20 minutes before carving it. (Letting it set will reduce the amount of juices flowing from the carved meat.) The carving begins with removing the skin with culinary scissors or any other tool(s) that work for you. It is likely that the skin will not be edible; it will likely be hard and have an unpleasant funky taste.

- After the skin is removed, carve and serve normally.

CHAPTER 10

Dry-Aged Lamb

ABOUT LAMBS AND LAMB MEAT

Important Point: This chapter provides information about dry-aged lamb. Chapter 12 will show you, step by step, how to dry age lamb or *any other kind of meat.*

Some of the countries in which sheep are commonly raised and eaten are Australia, United Kingdom, Canada, Ireland, the United States, numerous predominantly Islamic countries, and South Africa. Depending on the country, distinctions in sheep are sometimes made according to factors including the animal's age, sex, diet of the animal, and number of permanent incisors. Often, special vocabulary is used for lambs with these distinctions. Also, depending on the country, the method of separating the carcass into primal and sub-primal cuts differs.

When discussing sheep in this book, I will use the vocabulary that is common in the United States. For example, we generally consider a young sheep to be a *lamb* if it is less than 12 months of age. Also, *the meat* from a sheep that is less than 12 months old is called *lamb.*

Occasionally the words *baby lamb* and *spring lamb* are used here in the United States. *Baby lamb* is the meat from a 6- to 10-month-old animal, and *spring lamb* is usually from an animal 5 to 6 months old, though it may no longer mean that the animal was born in the spring or that it is associated with spring in any way!

Wholesale and retail marketers of lamb meat are no more angelic than are marketers of other products; they will sometimes describe products more favorably than warranted. For example, meat from sheep older than 12 months might be called *lamb* by some disreputable dealers.

A sheep between the age of one and two years old, or the meat from such a sheep, should be called *hogget*. Animals older than two years are simply called *sheep*, but meat from these older sheep is called *mutton*.

Lamb is naturally more tender and finer-grained than beef. It is also considered healthier than beef because there is less fat and less marbling, and the percentage of unsaturated fats is higher in lamb.

Lamb in the United States is divided into the following quality grades by the USDA (United States Department of Agriculture): *prime, choice, good, utility,* and *cull.* However, a supermarket will normally offer only prime and choice, and it should be kept in mind that USDA grading of lamb is not mandatory, so some cuts may be unmarked.

Finally, it is important to know that the lamb available in the United States is generally limited to that imported from Australia or New Zealand and the lamb produced here in the US. The lamb imported from Australia is similar to that from New Zealand, but it differs significantly from that produced in the US. To simplify comparison, the colloquialism *Down Under* may be used to replace *Australia and New Zealand* when discussing the lamb imported into the United States from these two countries. Lamb from Down Under is usually less expensive than that produced in the United States, but the best source of lamb is a matter for you to decide; it is strictly a matter of your personal preference.

SELECTING A CUT OF LAMB FOR DRY AGING

When selecting a cut of lamb for dry aging, the two most obvious matters to decide are the origin of the lamb (United States or Down Under) and the cut. Below, the difference between the lamb produced in the United States and that produced Down Under will be explained. Following that, the most suitable cuts of lamb for dry aging will be described.

COMPARING UNITED STATES, AUSTRALIAN, AND NEW ZEALAND LAMB

Down Under Lamb Meat

Lambs from Down Under are normally smaller than those raised in the United States. For example, a whole leg from a lamb imported from Australia or New Zealand may weigh only about 5 or 6 pounds (2.25–2.75 kg), whereas a leg from a US-raised lamb could weigh as much as 15 pounds (6.8 kg). The difference in size is due to both genetic differences and differences in diet.

The genetic differences, and the fact that the Down Under lambs usually have a 100 percent grass diet, causes this imported meat to taste decidedly gamy, makes it tougher, makes it drier, and results in a less rich flavor due to a lower fat content than the meat from American lambs.

On the other hand, it is a fact that many people are hooked on any kind of meat with a gamy taste. For them, the word *gamy* is drool-inducing. For them, the milder taste of the American lamb would be a disappointment.

If you're choosing whether to cook a Down Under leg or an American leg of lamb, the size of the leg may be the deciding factor. One Down Under lamb leg will provide about the right amount of meat for an average-sized family. One American lamb leg—if it is a large one—will feed two or three times that number of people.

Finally, the cheaper price per pound for the imported lamb might lead the budget-minded shopper to select the Down Under meat.

American Lamb Meat

Selective breeding and carefully planned animal husbandry have created lamb meat that more closely caters to the American taste. The American lamb normally has a less gamy taste, a richer flavor, and juicier meat. As mentioned above, selective breeding has helped to achieve this goal, but the diet is also important. (Some American ranchers raise their lambs on a 100 percent grass diet for the entire life of the animal, but the special "finishing diet" described below is more typical.)

Except for the last 30 days before the animal is harvested, the American lamb is typically grass-fed just as the Down Under lambs are. But during the last 30 days, the lamb is usually fed ("finished on") a predominantly grain diet. (Some of the lamb producers feed the animals a combination of grains that include wheat and flaked corn, and this blend of grains is often infused with honey and alfalfa.) Because this rich diet is limited to 30 days, there is not enough time for the animals to develop health problems, but the diet goes a long way to diminish the gamy taste of the meat caused by a 100 percent grass diet.

The primal cuts of the American lamb, especially the legs, have a thicker layer of protective fat than imported lambs. This fat makes the meat juicy and self-basting. Moreover, the fat is a great advantage if the meat is to be dry aged; it protects against the development of a hard, inedible rind, and it acts as a barrier and a shield to ward off bacteria and discourage mold.

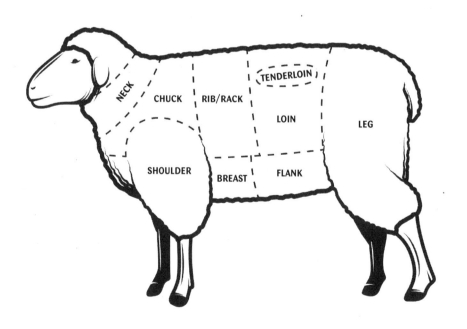

Lamb cuts.

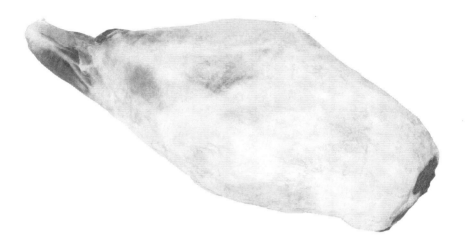

Whole leg of lamb with bone in. *Photo courtesy American Lamb Board.*

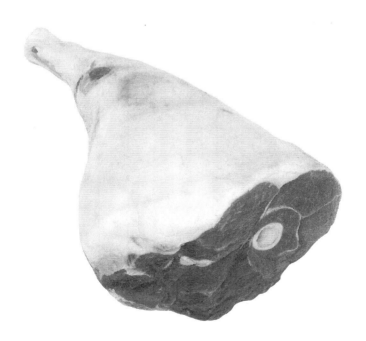

Leg of lamb, bone in, shank portion. *Photo courtesy American Lamb Board.*

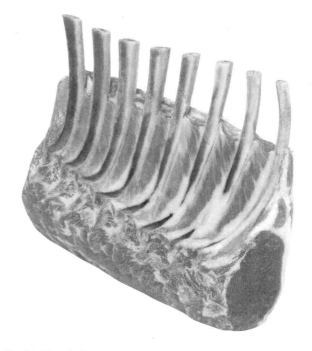

Rack of lamb, bone in. *Photo courtesy American Lamb Board.*

Lamb loin, bone in. *Photo courtesy American Lamb Board.*

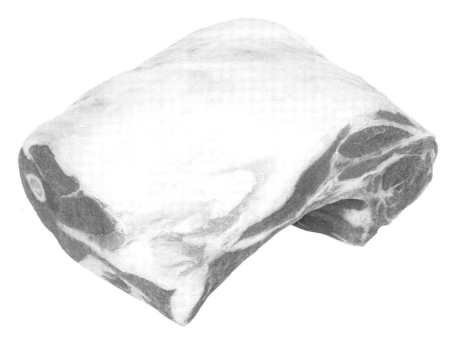

Whole lamb shoulder, square cut. *Photo courtesy American Lamb Board.*

THE BEST CUTS OF LAMB FOR DRY AGING

The reason for dry aging lamb or any other meat is explained in chapter 1: It makes the meat taste better and makes it more juicy and tender. The taste improvement of dry-aged lamb is similar to that of dry-aged beef; it creates an appealing nutty, cheesy, and intensified meaty flavor and aroma. However, the flavor change will not be as intense as with beef because lamb (and goat) cannot be dry aged as long as beef. This meat has a higher percent of unsaturated fat than beef, so it will become rancid faster than beef when exposed to oxygen during the dry-aging process.

The flavor improvements described above will be the same for any cut of lamb that is properly dry aged. The cuts described below, however, have certain advantages.

The most popular cuts of lamb for dry aging are the *leg of lamb* and the *rack of lamb*. The primary reason is that these are the cuts that will result in the highest percent of edible meat remaining after the aging is completed and the rind is trimmed and discarded. Below, the dry aging of these two primal cuts will be described and discussed.

Leg of Lamb

The *leg of the lamb* always refers to the rear leg. (The front leg is called the *shoulder.*) Leg of lamb for dry aging should always be *bone-in.* The reason for this is that much of *boned* meat—namely, the meat *inside* the leg and *near* the removed bone—will become so dry and hard that it will have to be wastefully trimmed off and discarded. Obviously, this waste of edible red meat will be avoided if the leg is not boned. Over-trimmed leg also causes waste; most of the fat on the leg should be left untrimmed to protect the underlying red meat.

The following are additional reasons why the leg should not be boned: If a *boned* leg of lamb is rolled-and-tied (or rolled-and-netted) in order to prevent the formation of rind, any bacteria inadvertently deposited on the inside muscle tissue during the bone extraction will be buried inside the leg during the entire aging process. This is definitely not good! It is almost a certainty that these bacteria will proliferate to dangerous levels because they will not be destroyed by the airflow inside the aging chamber (the refrigerator). It is quite possible for these bacteria to proliferate to the point that people who consume the meat become ill. If extreme proliferation of the bacteria resulted, it would cause the meat to rot. *Be safe: If a leg of lamb is to be dry aged, use a bone-in leg!*

Rack of Lamb

If rack of lamb is to be aged, a cut of meat called *rib roast* (also called *rack of lamb*) should be purchased. If the gristle-like flesh is trimmed off the base of each rib in order to expose about 3 inches (7.5 cm) of the bare bones, it is called a *Frenched rib roast.* Because most Americans consider rack of lamb to be the most desirable cut of lamb, it is the most expensive lamb in terms of price per pound. Also, the high bone-to-meat ratio further increases the cost of the *net* edible meat.

WHERE TO BUY LEG OF LAMB OR RACK OF LAMB

Depending on where you live, it might be difficult to find a meat market or a supermarket that offers leg of lamb or rack of lamb. Furthermore, a leg of lamb that has the bone in, is produced in the United States, and is fresh (has not been frozen) can be more difficult to find than frozen and boned leg of lamb imported from Australia or New Zealand. Also, a whole rack of lamb can be more difficult to find than a rack of lamb cut up into lamb chops.

Of course, almost anything can be ordered on the Internet nowadays, including lamb meat. However, it's very expensive, and you can probably find it locally with a little effort.

- Obviously, the larger the city and the greater the international diversity of the population, the easier it will be to find what you want. On an Internet search, you may see a reference to "**Islamic meat & poultry**" or words to this effect. Since the word *Islamic* is used, you can be sure that they will be selling lamb: Lamb and goat are the two most common meats that Islamic people are permitted to eat. These meats are considered *halal*, which means that they are acceptable under Islamic religious law. (Anytime you see the words *halal meat market*, you can be certain that they sell lamb and goat meat. I buy my lamb and goat meat at a nearby *halal* meat market in Beaverton, Oregon.)
- If you have no luck finding a nearby source on the Internet, go to the meat department in a supermarket and ask a friendly *professional* butcher if he or she knows where you can get the meat you want. Most good butchers would consider it a professional duty to help you find an acceptable source for an unusual joint of meat—even if they do not sell it in their own store.

ABOUT AGING AND COOKING AGED LAMB

The aging of lamb is certainly not as common as the aging of beef. In fact, there is no country in the world in which the dry aging of lamb is an established part of the culture. However, many people have come to realize that lamb is a red meat with a substantial fat cover, and the cuts of lamb mentioned above lend themselves very nicely to aging. In New York, a Korean family has attracted a large clientele to their restaurant (Prime & Beyond, East Village) that specializes in what is purported to be unbelievably delicious dry-aged lamb. In New Zealand, several small food shops sell dry-aged lamb by request.

One point to consider, however, is that beef contains a higher percent of saturated fats than lamb, so exposing lamb to air will cause it to become rancid sooner than beef. (Rancid meat will not make you sick, but it does have an unpleasant odor and taste.) This means that you will probably like your lamb to be aged a shorter length of time than beef. If you enjoy beef that has been aged 30 days, for example, you might wish to age your first batch of lamb 14 to 21 days.

The process for aging lamb is the same as the process for aging beef. Please refer to the step-by-step instructions in chapter 12.

The dry-aged leg of lamb, or rack of lamb, can be oven roasted using your favorite recipe, or it can be sliced into steaks or chops and grilled. If you do not have a favorite recipe for either roasting or grilling, you will find a wealth of recipes to choose from on the Internet; check *allrecipes.com*, for example. Rosemary, thyme, garlic, bay leaves, and onion are seasonings commonly used on roasted leg of lamb.

CHAPTER 11

Dry-Aged Goat

ABOUT GOATS AND GOAT MEAT

Important Point: This chapter provides information about dry-aged goat. Chapter 12 will show you, step by step, how to dry age goat or *any other kind of meat.*

It is likely that you have never dry aged goat meat and you wonder what to expect. In chapter 10, in the section *The Best Cuts of Lamb for Dry Aging,* you will find a paragraph that describes the improvements that can be brought about by dry aging lamb. All of these described improvements apply to goat—a relative of sheep.

Both the goat and the sheep belong to the same goat-antelope subfamily, and both were domesticated around 9000 BC. There are over 300 breeds of goats, and they have been used all over the world for their milk, meat, hair, and skins. Even here in the United States, goat cheese is becoming increasingly popular.

We will use no special vocabulary of French, Spanish, or Italian origin for goat meat. The meat will be called *young goat meat, kid meat,* or simply *goat meat.* Nevertheless, the meanings of the words of foreign origin need to be explained because English-speaking authorities on goat meat will often use these words:

- *Chevon,* a word derived from French, is used for the meat of adult goats. The British try to imitate the French pronunciation of *chevon,* but Americans will usually Americanize the pronunciation and pronounce it *shev'ən.*

- *Cabrito* is of Spanish origin and *capretto* is of Italian origin. Both words mean *"kid meat"* and are used occasionally in American English by specialists and by goat meat enthusiasts.

More than 70 percent of the world's people eat goat! It is, unbelievably, the most popular meat in the world, and it is a staple in Africa, Asia, South America, and Central America. A few European countries eat a substantial amount and consider it a delicacy. Historically, goat has been less popular in the United States, Canada, and Northern Europe. However, even in these geographic regions, goat meat has become increasingly popular in the areas that have received immigrants from Asian and African countries. In the United States, for example, goat meat is now being served in some of the white-tablecloth restaurants in San Francisco and New York.

There is a logical reason why goat meat has not become popular in United States, Canada, and Northern Europe: The goat has a thin layer of fur and little body fat. These two features mean that goats do not have enough protection against the cold and wet weather in our country, in Canada, or in Northern Europe. The goat is more comfortable in hot and arid climates.

Goat meat can be prepared by cooking it in the same way that other meats are prepared, and it can be made into sausage or jerky, as well. In Okinawa, it is sliced thin and served raw.

Just as with lamb, goat meat can have a gamy flavor, or it can have a mild one; it depends on how the animal was raised, the diet, and its age. Kids six to nine months old usually produce the best meat. Ribs, loins, and tenderloins can be cooked quickly, but other cuts need to be cooked slowly with low, moist heat. This is required not only because the other cuts of goat meat are tougher, but also because goat contains less fat than other meats such as beef and lamb.

SELECTING A CUT OF GOAT FOR DRY AGING

Selecting a cut of goat for dry aging is similar to selecting a cut of beef or lamb. It is wise to select a large cut that is thick. When the hunk of meat is thick, the area of flesh exposed to the air is small compared with the volume of flesh that is not exposed. The surface that is exposed to air will dry, harden, and become inedible rind, and that is trimmed off and usually discarded. Hence the obvious conclusion is

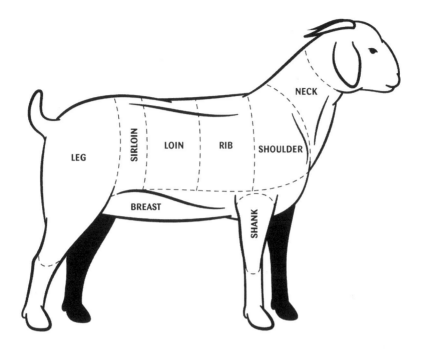

Goat cuts.

that the larger and thicker the cut of meat, the greater will be the percentage of edible meat.

The largest and thickest joint of meat on a kid is the rear leg, and the second largest joint would be the rack; the same is true for a lamb. Pictures of legs of lamb and a rack of lamb are in chapter 10. Because the best cuts of meat for a kid will look almost identical to those for the lamb, additional kid photos seemed to be superfluous and were not prepared. If necessary, please look at the corresponding lamb photos in chapter 10, *The Best Cuts of Lamb for Dry Aging.*

In my opinion, the most economical cut of kid for dry aging is the leg. The second best in terms of economy would probably be the rack, but it would likely result in a product tastier than a leg.

MEAT-GOAT BREEDS

As mentioned above, it is said that there are over 300 breeds of goats in the world. Even so, there are only about 10 commercially important breeds in the United States. Goat's milk has long been consumed in this country by people who are intolerant of cow's milk. It is believed that goat's milk is better tolerated because it is more similar to human milk than is cows' milk. Goat's milk is increasingly used to make many kinds of goat cheese, which are rapidly gaining popularity in the United States.

Because the dairy-goat industry is bigger than the meat-goat industry in the United States, the most numerous type of goats are six breeds of dairy goats. The names of these breeds are not important, but it is interesting to note that the excess kids, especially male kids, are often slaughtered and sold as meat kids. This happens especially at Easter time. (Excess kids are a by-product of the dairy-goat industry; in order for a doe to give milk, she must first give birth to a kid, and if the kid is a baby buck, he is of no use to the industry except for stud service. Consequently, male kids were often put down at birth, but the increasing demand for goat meat now encourages ranchers to raise them as meat goats.)

Because of the increasing interest in goat meat in the United States, true meat goats—goats that are meatier than dairy goats—are now being raised in increasing numbers this country.

Boer goat. The Boer goat was developed in the early 1900's in South Africa. It is one of the most common breeds of meat goat.

The following are considered meat goats:

- **South African Boer Goat:** It is believed that this South African breed is the result of the crossbreeding of Bantu tribe native goats and Asian goats brought into South Africa by Dutch immigrants. In the 1980s, the local goat ranchers in South Africa began selective breeding to produce a good meat goat, and this newly recognized breed was introduced into the Unites States in the 1990s. They have a reputation for outstanding weight gain and large carcasses.
- **Spanish Meat Goat:** These goats are descended from those brought to the United States by the early settlers in New England. They gradually migrated south into Texas, where they interbred with goats that early Spanish settlers brought to America. Ranchers gradually selected the best of these "mongrel" goats for meat production.
- **Tennessee Meat Goat:** In Tennessee in 1880, a flock of goats with an abnormal muscle condition was discovered. This abnormality causes their muscles to lock up for about 10 seconds whenever they are startled, and this stiffening of the muscles often causes them to fall over. Technically speaking, they are known as *myotonic goats*, and this muscle condition is called *myotonia*. Some ranchers in Texas bred the larger and heavier of these goats, and they came to be known as *Tennessee meat goats*. It is believed that this muscle condition causes the goats to have larger and more tender rear leg muscles.
- **New Zealand Kiko Goat:** In New Zealand, feral does (wild females) were bred with Saanen and Nubian bucks to make a better dairy goat. Then the largest and the meatiest of these crossbred goats were bred in order to develop a good meat goat.

If you buy your goat from a *ranch* that specializes in raising these meat goats, you can obtain the meat from one of these breeds. However, if you buy from a *shop* that deals in goat meat, you may not be able to determine, with certainty, whether the meat is from a dairy breed animal or a meat breed animal.

WHERE TO BUY LEG OF GOAT OR RACK OF GOAT

Finding a place to buy leg of goat or rack of goat is similar to finding a place to by lamb. One big difference is that lamb can sometimes be found in supermarkets, but the only grocery store that might have goat is something like an international grocery store or an ethnic food store.

If you will kindly refer to the section in chapter 10, *Where to Buy Leg of Lamb or Rack of Lamb*, you will find some search suggestions that are equally applicable for finding goat meat.

ABOUT AGING GOAT

In chapter 10, *Dry-Aged Lamb*, it was pointed out that the aging of lamb meat is certainly not as common as the aging of beef. The same statement applies to the dry aging of goat. Also, no country in the world dry ages goat as an established part of the culture. Nevertheless, there are goat ranchers and goat meat aficionados all over the world, including the United States, who are discovering that dry-aged goat meat is delicious.

As mentioned above, all of the primal cuts of goat have less fat—marbled and external—than lamb or beef. Consequently, there will be less superficial fat available to reduce rind formation of the edible red meat, and there will be fewer flecks and streaks of fat (marbling) within the lean sections of meat.

Because fat is sparse on goat meat, more red meat is exposed to air on the surface of goat meat than on the surface of lamb and other meats. This means that more meat is lost to rind trimming with goat than with fattier kinds of meat.

Because goat has fewer flecks and streaks of fat in the muscle tissue, it's normally drier than lamb. On the other hand, as was previously explained, dry aging makes the meat juicier because the dry-aging process reduces shrinkage when meat is cooked. This dry-aging benefit helps to compensate for dearth of marbling.

Of course, the same dry-aging process that is used for beef can also be used for kid. However, you may wish to make the aging period a week or so less than the number of days you like to age beef; this is because goat fat is less saturated than beef fat. Hence, aging of goat may lead to rancidity more quickly than the aging of beef.

The dry-aged goat can be sliced into steaks or chops and grilled, or it can be oven roasted, for example. Recipes for cooking goat meat are nonexistent or scarce in most American cookbooks, but you will find numerous mouthwatering recipes on the Internet; check *allrecipes.com*, for example. If you happen to have a lamb recipe that is your favorite, using kid meat in place of lamb should produce a very similar result.

CHAPTER 12

Step-by-Step Dry Aging

A CHECKLIST FOR DRY AGING MEAT

The basic dry-aging instructions are listed below to show you the big picture for dry aging various meats. The procedure for dry aging is very easy and is almost identical for all meats, so it is most efficient to put the instructions in this one small chapter.

The following information pool and checklist *can and should* be considered a kind of template for developing a personal checklist that will be even more useful for you. These instructions *can, and should,* be modified and refined to meet the variables in your situation: your preferences, the available raw materials, your equipment, your budget, and more—the variables are numerous.

It would likely be helpful for you to put together a three-ring binder that holds a personalized information cache about dry aging. It can be purposefully compiled and indexed so that it is meaningful to you and addresses your personal concerns. For example, the following topics and indexes might be useful: dry-aging times and techniques for various meats that are of special interest to you; local butcher-shop phone numbers and butchers' names; favorite meat recipes; and much more information tailored to meet your special needs.

Most of the steps for dry aging—from the very beginning to the finish—are listed below. The ordering of the steps is obviously important in some cases and unimportant in other cases. Some steps that seem to be patently common sense were omitted.

- Gather the basic equipment required for dry aging. Most of these items are described in chapter 2, *Equipment*. Some examples of the items required are as follows: a refrigerator, cleaning equipment and supplies, knives, pans, devices to measure the temperature and humidity of the refrigerator interior, cooking thermometers, and poultry shears. Additional cooking equipment and supplies will be required if you will be the person who cooks the dry-aged meats.
- After the equipment is purchased and gathered, it is wise to do some testing. For example, if you purchased a *wireless indoor/outdoor thermo-hygrometer and transponder* as recommended, you should read the instructions and practice using it to control the temperature and the humidity of your dry-aging refrigerator while it is empty. This exercise is enormously beneficial: It tests these important measuring instruments, calibrates your refrigerator, gives you self-confidence, and may prevent the loss of a hunk of meat that cost you over a hundred dollars.
- While you are testing your *wireless indoor/outdoor thermo-hygrometer and transponder*, you can decide on the placement of your air circulation fan(s), and make sure that your water dish (for humidity control) fits in an appropriate refrigerator space.
- The cleaning equipment and supplies mentioned above will be used mainly to sanitize the dry-aging chamber (the refrigerator) prior to each dry-aging session. Good sanitation is very important for dry aging; this importance is explained in chapter 3, *Health Matters*. Chapter 4 describes how professional cleaners of food service equipment would clean a refrigerator used for dry aging. If these step-by-step instructions are followed, you will have the benefit of their professional expertise, and you will do a perfect job in the shortest possible time. This refrigerator sanitation

job should be done before buying the meat to be dry aged. *Hint:* If the temperature of the refrigerator has been tested and adjusted, try to avoid moving the temperature adjustment dial while cleaning; if the dial is *not* moved, it is likely that the time-consuming readjustment of the refrigerator can be avoided. (If the internal-temperature-control dial was moved during cleaning, several days might be required to readjust and stabilize the temperature.)

- Before you buy a hunk of meat to dry age, you should read chapters 1 through 5 in this book. Actually, in this chapter, we have already touched upon much of the material in chapters 1 through 4, but it would be best to absorb some of the technical aspects of dry aging that is presented in chapter 5. Having a fundamental knowledge of dry-aging technology gives you a clear understanding of the process.

- After exposure to most of the material in chapter 5, *it is time for the fun to begin.* It's time to go buy a hunk of meat and begin dry aging it. Well, it's almost time for the fun to begin. I forgot about a few more things to do before you leave for the butcher shop.

- Before you buy the meat, you will need to measure the inside of your refrigerator to decide the maximum length of the hunk. If, for example, your refrigerator is 16 inches (40.5 cm) from the inside of the left wall to the inside of the right wall, then the maximum length permissible for the meat is 14 inches (35.5 cm). That's because a minimum of 1 inch (2.5 cm) of space is required all around the meat to allow for the free flow of the air.

- Now decide on the variety of meat you want to dry age. Do you want to dry age beef, lamb, elk, duck, or something else? Next, you will need to decide on the cut of meat— though this isn't required if you have already decided on duck, for example. Deciding on the cut of meat is one of the most important decisions, because each cut has unique features. If you are considering beef, then consult *Selecting a Cut of Beef* in chapter 6 to help you decide. In fact, it would be a good idea to read all of chapter 6 and study the importance of things such as the fat cap and chine. Much of the information provided about beef and beef cuts also applies to meat from other animals.

- If you wish to dry age a duck, read all of chapter 8 from beginning to end, and pay special attention to the role of the duck skin in the process.

- Do you like lamb? Detailed information for dry aging lamb is in chapter 10.

- If Aussies wished to age kangaroo, they would not go wrong by using a roo loin or a roo rack and following the dry-aging instructions—more or less—for goat or lamb.

- If I were to do the rear leg of a young pig, I would dry age it as a leg of lamb, but I would leave all of the skin and fat on it and increase the aging time to about 30 days. The skin and most of the fat would be removed and discarded prior to cooking. There are countless recipes suitable for dry-aged pork. In fact, just about any recipe for pork would work very well with dry-aged pork.

- I often telephone my meat market or butcher shop in advance to make sure they can fill my needs. If they can't, I select something else to dry age or decide to wait till I can find a supplier for my first choice. As previously mentioned, an independent butcher shop is more likely to be able to supply your needs than the meat department in a big-box grocery store. (The big-box grocery store usually does not have a good selection of *large* cuts of meat, and the meat is often trimmed excessively.) The meat available in a common big-box grocery store is that which is commonly eaten in households, and, except for roasts, it's often cut into individual servings, not large primal and subprimal cuts.

- It is a good idea to use a timer to help you remember to do certain chores. These chores are mingled throughout the dry-aging process. A timer was not mentioned on the special equipment list because so many households have one, but it is very useful for dry aging. For example, a timer helps you to remember to baste marinated meat several times a day; it helps you remember to check the refrigerator temperature and humidity from time to time; and the list goes on.

- After the temperature and humidity of your sparkling-clean refrigerator have been stabilized, and after the newly purchased meat has been trimmed (if required or desired), *the fun continues*. The big hunk of meat (or the bird) is placed on a wire rack in the dry-aging chamber (aka refrigerator). The object is to control the temperature and humidity and leave the refrigerator door closed as much as possible until the dry-aging time has ended. Your main activity at this time is to monitor the temperature and humidity in the fridge while doing things such as watching TV, reading a book, or knitting a sweater for your pet iguana. Occasionally, you may need take necessary action to maintain the established temperature and humidity parameters. Assuming that there are no disasters such as power failures, "taking necessary action" is normally doing things like making a minor adjustment in the temperature control of the refrigerator, or playing horseshoes with your grandson so he won't repeatedly open the doggone dry-aging refrigerator.

- Also, the dry-aging meat needs to be turned over occasionally to ensure that a uniform flow of drying air is passing over all surfaces. Turn the meat over daily during the first 3 days, and turn it over every other day for the next 10 days. After that, it's usually adequate to turn the meat over once every three days.

- The dry-aging time ends at a previously decided date or when certain indicators (mentioned in the various chapters of this book) prescribe that it should be terminated. (For birds, the pinch test is one of those indicators.) Until the dry aging is finished, the door is opened only for mandatory tasks such as turning the meat over, refilling the water dish, and the like. (Of course, it is permissible to open the door *for a few seconds* to allow a peek by the next-door neighbor or a relative, especially if they seem to be awed by your dry-aging activities.)

- When you decide that the dry aging is finished, remove the meat from the refrigerator, shave off the rind, trim appropriately, and begin cooking it. The plans for cooking and the recipe, if any, should have been decided while the meat was dry aging. Enjoy!

Fahrenheit < > Celsius Conversion Table

F°	to	C°	F°	to	C°	F°	to	C°
-30	=	-34.4	150	=	65.6	330	=	165.6
-25	=	-31.7	155	=	68.3	335	=	168.3
-20	=	-28.9	160	=	71.1	340	=	171.1
-15	=	-26.1	165	=	73.9	345	=	173.9
-10	=	-23.3	170	=	76.7	350	=	176.7
-5	=	-20.6	175	=	79.4	355	=	179.4
0	=	-17.8	180	=	82.2	360	=	182.2
5	=	-15.0	185	=	85.0	365	=	185.0
10	=	-12.2	190	=	87.8	370	=	187.8
15	=	-9.4	195	=	90.6	375	=	190.6
20	=	-6.7	200	=	93.3	380	=	193.3
25	=	-3.9	205	=	96.1	385	=	196.1
30	=	-1.1	210	=	98.9	390	=	198.9
35	=	1.7	215	=	101.7	395	=	201.7
40	=	4.4	220	=	104.4	400	=	204.4
45	=	7.2	225	=	107.2	405	=	207.2
50	=	10.0	230	=	110.0	410	=	210.0

(continued)

F°	to	C°	F°	to	C°	F°	to	C°
55	=	12.8	235	=	112.8	415	=	212.8
60	=	15.6	240	=	115.6	420	=	215.6
65	=	18.3	245	=	118.3	425	=	218.3
70	=	21.1	250	=	121.1	430	=	221.1
75	=	23.9	255	=	123.9	435	=	223.9
80	=	26.7	260	=	126.7	440	=	226.7
85	=	29.4	265	=	129.4	445	=	229.4
90	=	32.2	270	=	132.2	450	=	232.2
95	=	35.0	275	=	135.0	455	=	235.0
100	=	37.8	280	=	137.8	460	=	237.8
105	=	40.6	285	=	140.6	465	=	240.6
110	=	43.3	290	=	143.3	470	=	243.3
115	=	46.1	295	=	146.1	475	=	246.1
120	=	48.9	300	=	148.9	480	=	248.9
125	=	51.7	305	=	151.7	485	=	251.7
130	=	54.4	310	=	154.4	490	=	254.4
135	=	57.2	315	=	157.2	495	=	257.2
140	=	60.0	320	=	160.0	500	=	260.0

$F = ((9/5)C) + 32 \qquad C = (5/9)(F\text{-}32)$

APPENDIX 2

Weight and Volume Conversion Tables

Metric equivalents for US weight and volume measurements are indicated all through the body of this book. The measurements are not always precisely converted, but the conversion accuracy is sufficient to produce essentially the same result. Precise conversion would result in very awkward measurements, and it might require brain-numbing calculations. Such precision is not needed.

The Imperial (UK) units of measurement are not mentioned in the body of this book for two reasons. The first is that metric units are replacing these units rapidly. The second is that great confusion could result because the words used for Imperial units of measurement are often the same words used for the US units, even though the actual quantity may be different. (Countries that are, or were, part of the British Commonwealth and have officially converted to metric may or may not retain the Imperial definition of non-metric measurement units; metric units should always be used for these countries.) You may assume the *weight* measurements in the British system to be the same as those in the US system: A pound in this system of measurement is the same as a US pound. If it is a *volume* measurement, you should assume that it is different from the US system: An Imperial gallon, for example is not the same as a US gallon.

If you need additional help to covert one measurement to another system, there are several excellent Internet websites. Simply do a Google search for: "Convert inches to metric," or vice versa.

Weight Conversion Table

	ounce(s)	pound(s)	gram(s)	kilogram(s)
1 ounce	1	$\frac{1}{16}$	28.35	0.028
1 pound	16	1	454	0.454
1 gram	0.032	0.002	1	0.001
1 kilogram	0.000032	2.2	1000	1

Volume and Fluid Conversions: US < > Metric

This table does not represent precise conversions: 1 cup actually equals 236 ml, and 1 gallon equals 3,785.4 ml, for example. However, for most culinary purposes, such precision is meaningless. The table presented below is quite easy to commit to memory, it is easy to calculate, and its accuracy is sufficient.

US System	Metric (ml)	Metric (Liters)
⅛ teaspoon	0.625 ml	
¼ teaspoon	1.25 ml	
½ teaspoon	2.5 ml	
¾ teaspoon	3.75 ml	
1 teaspoon	5 ml	
1 tablespoon (3 teaspoons)	15 ml	
1 fluid ounce (2 tablespoons)	30 ml	
¼ cup (4 tablespoons)	60 ml	
½ cup (8 tablespoons)	120 ml	
¾ cup (12 tablespoons)	180 ml	
1 cup (16 tablespoons)	240 ml	0.24 Liter
1 pint (2 cups) (16 fluid ounces)	480 ml	0.48 Liter
1 quart (4 cups) (32 fluid ounces)	960 ml	0.96 Liters
1 gallon (4 quarts)	3,840 ml	3.840 Liters

Conversion of the British Volume Measuring System

It is impossible to convert, with confidence, the British volume measuring system to either the metric volume measurement system or the American volume measuring system. For example, some conversion tables or conversion programs state that one UK teaspoon is equal to about 3.5 ml, and some state that one UK teaspoon is equal to about 5.9 ml.

There is no good solution to this dilemma. Usually the source cannot be consulted, so the only option is to record the metric equivalent used and make changes if the result is not acceptable.

APPENDIX 3

Cooking Chart

The following meat-cooking chart may be useful. It is intended to be used for all varieties of meat that can safely be eaten rare. This information was taken from an American reference book, but gradations and the associated temperature ranges—even within the United States—vary regionally from cuisine to cuisine and with local customs. Consequently, the sole purpose of this chart is to explain the generally accepted meaning of the words *rare, medium rare,* et cetera.

Obviously, it is always best to use the temperature range in degrees, whenever possible, rather than depend on interpreting a word that describes a range. If the actual temperature range is not stated, and you do not have the experience to decide your preference, the use of this chart—or a similar chart—may be necessary. If you do have a preference—if you know, for example, that you like lamb cooked to between 130 and 140° F (54.4–60.0°C), then it is best to cook it to that temperature despite what the recipe says.

Description	°F and °C
Rare	125–130°F (51.7–54.4°C)
Medium rare	130–140°F (54.4–60.0°C)
Medium	140–150°F (60.0–65.6°C)
Medium well	150–155°F (65.6–68.3°C)
Well done	160°F (71.1°C) and above

Index